R.A.W.

RELEASE ALL WITHIN
TRANSFORMATION

R.A.W.

RELEASE ALL WITHIN TRANSFORMATION

RELEASE PAST EXPERIENCES HINDERING YOUR NEXT LEVEL OF ELEVATION

THIS BOOK IS DESIGNED TO HELP YOU
PURGE | EMERGE | SURGE

PURGE=RID OF UNWANTED FEELINGS | EMERGE=MANIFEST ONESELF |
SURGE=POWERFUL UPWARD MOVEMENT

NATASHAY STARR
Certified Transformational Coach & Speaker

FREE GIFT
SCAN CODE

TRANSFORMATIONAL RETREATS | TRANSFORM U PROGRAMS
MENTORSHIP PROGRAMS | CUSTOMIZED WORKSHOPS

LET'S CONNECT AT THE NEXT EVENT!

🅵 🅸 ♪ lamnatashaystarr

ISBN: 979-8-9896697-0-7- Paperback
ISBN: 979-8-9896697-1-4- Hardcover
eISBN: 979-8-9896697-2-1- eBook

Library of Congress Control Number: 2024901018

♾This paper meets the requirements of ANSI/NISO Z39.48-1992 (Permanence of Paper

020124

This book is a true part of my destiny! I have been blocked, stopped, and distracted from finishing this book several times. Over a twenty-year journey, with eight years of distraction, it took over three years to write and complete this purposeful book. A delay is not a denial! How often do we allow our destiny to be detoured by distractions?

My purpose, my destiny, and part of my legacy are linked to this book.
I am honored to provide a complete product of purpose!

First, I would like to thank my Heavenly Father, God of the universe, and my Guardian Angels and Heavenly entities that led me to a place of passion and purpose. Special express gratitude goes to the Butterfly Girlz: my daughter/ride-or-die, Genesis "RoyalGE" Jean, my mother/sister/best friend, Lana L. Forte, and my grandmother, the matriarch, Rosa J. Hamilton (rest in peace). Each one of us has been through the dark cocoon together and now we are flying high like butterflies!

I also honor my dad, Charles D. Green, -an extraordinary man, and his lovely wife, Jo Green.

Detailed dedications are located at the end of the book. This is my first book, therefore everyone who was instrumental in my journey is listed in the acknowledgments. This dedication is lengthy and unorthodox. However, I had to give written accolades to those who started my journey with me. Some people were in my life for a season, reason, or lifetime! Nevertheless, I will always have agape love for you!

May God bless everyone and their future endeavors.

A professional thank-you for assisting me with my first book:
Bishop Patrick Ivey, Ira Blount, Donna Cager, Genesis RoyalGE Jean, and Lana Forte, M.Ed.

*THANK YOU
I APPRECIATE YOUR SUPPORT.*

*WELCOME TO THE R.A.W. TRANSFORMATIONAL
JOURNEY OF PURGING, EMERGING, THEN
SURGING INTO YOUR WHOLENESS!*

CONTENTS

PREFACE

Have you ever experienced disappointments, dilemmas, setbacks, mishaps, heartbreaks, pain, or unbearable emotional meltdowns? We believe we will get stronger over the years and find ways to bypass life's trials and tribulations, the torture of unseen micro mechanisms that have caused us to build invisible walls, electric fences with barbed wire around our heart, mind, and spirit, causing our physical body to resemble a zombie. You no longer recognize yourself and start wondering, why do I still exist? If this sounds familiar, this is your new beginning.

After years of suppressing secrets and self-medicating I knew I had to make a change. I started my personal self-reflection in the early 2000s. I took a hiatus from everyone and everything around me and started to deeply analyze my broken life. Everyone around me called me a hermit. Divinely, I was offered a job in California that allowed me to truly isolate from others. Finally, in the mid-2000s, each piece of my puzzle began to come together to provide a complete version of myself, Natashay Starr. Yes, I am still growing, changing, and elevating into a person I love! Do you love yourself? Do you know yourself? Are you willing to become transparent? Do you have the desire to change?

I invite you on a transformational journey to purge your past, emerge into the present, and surge into your wholeness! It is time to go R.A.W.—Release All Within.

CHAPTER 1

RAPE IS REAL

Have you ever kept a deep, dark secret for so long that even you forgot about it? A secret you suppressed way down in your memory bank in the deepest crevices of your membranes and soul that unknowingly was the very thing that changed the course of your life? We may keep a variety of secrets, some not as excruciating as others. What about the secret of being raped, molested, abused, tortured, taken advantage of without your consent? This torture can be inflicted from people we love and trust, such as a beloved family member or friend, or a foe, an influential leader, someone in a position of esteemed power, or even a stranger.

This chapter will not determine who is right or wrong, it will simply identify how people who experience abuse have lived with a closed mouth, in silence, for years. Why the silence? Why have you been quiet about painful and shameful things that happened to you? I encourage you to research the statistics of how many people undergo abuse. Could you imagine being able to heal from your experience and pay it forward by helping others heal?

In order to free myself from the very secret that held me captive, I had to relive my past to purge my pain, guilt, and the heavy weights keeping me anchored. Imagine a cruise ship dropping a huge anchor into the middle of the ocean so the boat will not move. Your anchor might not be rape, but we all have trauma that has changed the course of our life and held us down. I want you to think of your personal story, your secret that no one knows about or very few know about and write down your truth. Some stories are more horrific than others, but own your personal pain, no matter how others might view it. This is your life, your hurt, your pain. Your goal is to elevate yourself, so you must eliminate the waste of your past to surge into your purpose.

Join me in my journey as I relive one of my stories. There is power in transparency and healing in truth.

~~~

Get off me!!!! Stop!!!! Leave me alone!!!! HELP!!!! Call 911!!!! STOP!!!! I'm yelling at the top of my lungs and my best friend is in the other room with her boyfriend trying to kick the door in. She's saying, "Leave my friend alone!" "What are y'all doing?" "*STOP!*" Then everything goes silent. My friend is no longer banging on the door, and I'm left to endure the turmoil alone . . .

The night was NOT supposed to end this way. Originally, we were all supposed to get together and have some fun. My bestie's boyfriend had invited his friends over so we could meet and greet while playing cards and dominoes. I've done this before, a couple of friends introducing each other to see if any of us are possibly compatible. Normally, a person just invites one guy—not a posse of three, yes three, friends. My best friend's boyfriend was of legal age, so he brought beer, wine, and liquor with him and offered us some flavored booze. At the time, I was too young to drink, and I hated the taste of alcohol. I'd tried some before and it was nasty. My friend and I did not drink, but we wanted to act grown, hell, we even lied about our age. Besides, I came from a family of alcoholics, and I vowed to NEVER be like some of my family members (never say never—but that's for another time and another chapter), so I sipped the nectar.

The flavored booze, for some reason, tasted like a delicious tropical drink. There was no warning of the aftereffect. We sipped it slowly but steady like two grown adults. When the guys arrived, I had a half glass left and I already felt sick. My head was spinning, my stomach twisting and turning, and my gag reflex kept activating as if I was about to vomit. Although I was underage, I tried to be grown. I didn't fully understand the consequences of drinking, especially around horny men. Honestly, I thought men only behaved like wild, horny animals on movies or television. Though I still felt sick, I was able to maintain my decorum and I continued to drink. The flavorful drink tasted good. Unfortunately, I learned a valuable lesson the hard way.

I was dressed like T-Boz from the group TLC with baggy jeans, a short shirt, and name brand boots. My hair was jet black, slicked down with gel, and styled in a long, around-the-way ponytail. I sported a huge gold chain and big hoop earrings. Yes, I looked like a true celebrity, and I felt like a boss. The scrub-looking guys were not the type of guys I liked at all. Honestly, they just looked grimy. As street smart as I thought I was, I didn't think guys could be so bold and malicious. I know robbers rob, thieves steal, but I never thought men could be so violent and careless. Still feeling no fear, I made it clear I was only here to play card games. The guys kept trying to talk to me, but I was not interested in any of them. My bestie and I acted like we were already in a relationship if we were not feeling someone. At the time, my friend had the best one out of all the guys; the other three were not polished and, frankly, looked like thugs. Don't get me wrong, I used to like men with a thug side to them, but with a corporate appeal, especially entre-preneurs who owned a successful business. Fittingly, I called these type of guys Corporate-Thugs. Boy, have I changed. Either way, none of the guys appealed to me. The three amigos didn't seem like they would harm anyone—not enough to feel like I was in danger—just enough to hide your purse or wallet because they might take your moolah.

"SHUT HER UP!!!" "COVER HER MOUTH!" What the hell was happening? It happened so fast! I went to vomit the flavored liquor out of my system and use the ladies' room. Once I walked out it was like three bulldogs scooped me up, covered my mouth, and took me into the other room. I was thrown & tossed around in a dark room and my clothes were ripped off me. One hand held my throat, another held my right ankle, and a third held my left ankle. Both of my hands were held by the first guy who forced himself on top of me. *NO! STOP! Get OFF of me!* I'm normally a praying woman, but I couldn't even call out to Jesus. What was happening? I heard belt buckles being undone and pants dropping. As he began to rip off my panties, my worst nightmare was realized.

The first one pounded, pounded, pounded me so hard he ripped through my tightly woven walls as I screamed as loud as I could—*"HELP ME!"* He covered my mouth and told me he would kill me if I did not cooperate. He pounded me as if he was pounding ground beef to make sure all the seasonings penetrated through the core. Each thrust pounded the life out of me. I heard others laughing and talking about how it was their turn. How many were there? After he finished pounding me, the others fought for their turn to rape me. I kept blacking out. All I could hear was them fighting for their turn. They were laughing and bragging about how they f**ked the sh*t out of me.

As I was recapping my life, I didn't know what guy was on top of me, but I knew I was going to mess somebody up after this was done—we had guns and all I could think about was shooting all of them between the legs so they could never harm another female. I was crying from the man pounding on top of me and the pounding in my heart from it being broken. As he was ripping my insides out with his huge penis, I blacked out again.

I was awakened by sweat dripping down on me—gross! This dude was fat and he was sweating all over me like he was in a sauna. Gross! Were they using condoms? Did they have any diseases? Who were these thugs? Would I live? Would they kill me afterward? Should I tell my mom or anyone? Oh, thank goodness he was done, at least with the physical abuse. I did not realize the mental anguish would last a lifetime.

My turn, my turn, they saved the best for last. I know that sounds strange, but it was true. He was gentle; my vagina was so sore and raw, but somehow, he massaged it in circles and it felt soothing. His voice did not have an American accent; he was from an island, I did not know which one. I wanted to scream, fight, kick, and scratch like I did the others. I could not believe I was actually moaning. Was I delusional? Him raping me did not feel like a rape? Are you being raped if you enjoy the act? I felt so ashamed that I felt a connection with my third rapist. It was a sick, sad, broken day in my life. I left my friend's boyfriend's house with my head down and my pride, respect, and vagina in pain.

I wanted to kill them. I truly felt so defeated that I went into a shell instead of lashing out. I hugged my mom and I did not tell her, I did not tell anyone; I made my best friend promise to never speak of this night again. I went to the clinic and got tested for all diseases and pregnancy, and I was thankful to be healthy. As a teenager and through most of my adult life, I kept this secret locked inside of me and made myself forget. I thought not talking about it would help me forget it happened. Well, hurt people hurt people. I took out my pain on other people unknowingly, and I hurt some nice men. I apologized to them later after seeking professional help because my rape experience broke me internally. I had other episodes that contributed to my brokenness, so it was time to evaluate my life and unapologetically reveal my secret pain, in order to what? Yes, purge my past!

In closing, once any unorthodox act is done to hurt you, unfortunately, you feel violated and a part of you is shut off from trust. My story kept me in bondage for way too long! Yes, it was painful and tragic, and it had me questioning God, my friend, and mankind. Who could I trust? I shut down for years! I changed without fully noticing my change, but I treated men mean for years. As an adult I did seek professional counseling to release the pain and anger I felt toward my abusers so I could heal and be able to forgive my tormentors. I took a forgiveness class as well!

Use this section to analyze any similar aspects of your life. Identify your pain! Yes, take time to analyze your experience and remove toxins from your bloodstream and increase your oxygen level so you can breathe and live your life more freely each day. Layer by layer own your pain so you can perpetuate your life's purpose.

Now, not everyone is the victim. Some people are identified as the oppressor, the bully, the one causing the pain. If you are the one who caused others pain, it is never too late to change. If this is you, I challenge all oppressors who caused harm to another individual to make amends. An apology is therapeutic and healing. When we hold on to past pain, these secrets will haunt you, too. I took a forgiveness class and it helped me realize there is power in forgiving and asking for forgiveness. But to deny that we either experienced, caused, or received pain can cause us to develop internal illnesses. Now is the time to Release All Within and surge into your wholeness.

CHAPTER 1 SELF-EVALUATION AND NOTES

1) Have you experienced rape or nonconsensual sexual abuse? Yes or No?

_____

_____

_____

_____

_____

_____

_____

2) Who corrupted you?

_____

_____

_____

_____

_____

_____

_____

3) Did you tell anyone? If so, who?

4) How did this act affect you?

5) Have you released your anger from your experience? If so, how?

_____

_____

_____

_____

_____

_____

_____

Notes

_____

_____

_____

_____

_____

_____

_____

_____

*Call the rape and/or abused crises hotline if you need assistance. See the Resources section for organizations that can help. Remember they are equipped for your situation. They have heard it all, from biological family members, pastors, friends, celebrities, authoritative figures, and unknowns violating trust. It's a No-Judgment Zone!

Purge: Get rid of unwanted feelings

Emerge: Rise from the situation

Surge: Propel your pain into power and purpose

Assignment: Write how you will PURGE, EMERGE, then SURGE.

_____

_____

_____

_____

_____

_____

_____

_____

_____

_____

_____

_____

_____

_____

National Sexual Assault Hotline:

1-800-656-HOPE (4673)

CHAPTER 2
VICES VARY

When you experience a dreadful day—work wars, money issues, relationship dilemmas, spiritual crises, racial tension, death, abuse, or you're just miserable with yourself or your overall life—how do you overcome your daily crises? Do you work out, play sports, pray, meditate, or maintain a kumbaya attitude by managing the cards you are dealt with a winning attitude? If so, good for you! You are such a role model and inspiration to others! However, if you use vices (alcohol, drugs, sex, etc.) to cope with your daily challenges, you will identify with this chapter.

First remove all myths and judgments about who uses vices and who does not. We are dealing with your truth, and if you have certain stereotypes embedded in your head about how one should look, then you might overlook your truth. A vice does not discriminate. It provides a feeling that surpasses outer appearances and gratifies each individual differently. I had to remove my own misperceptions in order to see that a vice was taking me over slowly and consuming me.

So, I ask you, is there a gratifying vice that gives you great pleasure? Is it alcohol, food, legal and/or illegal drugs, sexual fetishes, lying, cheating, bad habits that make you feel good? The list really goes on and on, because with over seven billion people in the world each have their very own DNA and may or may not have a vice to mask their hidden idiosyncrasy. With this high population, the vice possibilities are endless. Vices vary. It is a me, myself, and I moment of truth. Honesty is the best policy, especially to yourself! Do you have a vice that is hard to overcome? Did you know the first step, which happens to be the hardest step, is admitting you are powerless over a vice or vices? No one can tell another person they have a problem—the truth must start from within you.

We must remove the myth that a person must look a certain way when they become addicted to their vice. People discriminate, not vices! Addiction can happen to anyone regardless of their income, ethnicity, age, or upbringing. Remove all these myths. Anyone can become addicted to a vice! For some reason I had to learn that the hard way. I did not think a vice could take hold of me because I saw the damage, firsthand, in the area of alcoholism and what it did to my family, both privately and embarrassingly so, in public.

Alcoholism runs through my family. This disease caused family feuds, excessive piss-poor behavior, sexual, emotional, and physical abuse, repeated financial burdens, and premature death. I thought since I knew the damage alcohol could cause; it would not happen to me. My vices started out unbeknownst to me because it was a vice I never thought would sneak up on me. You think you can outsmart your DNA. Since I came from a long line of alcoholics, it was NEVER going to happen to me. Well, never say never!

When I got older, I began to sip on occasions. There was no true method to my drinking, I was just a social drinker. If someone took me on a date, we would drink. Girls' day, we would drink. At parties, we would drink. If I was sad, I would drink; happy, I would drink. Holidays, I would drink; birthdays, I would drink. You get my drift? My fun was based on my drink of the day. I started to notice every activity included drinking. It didn't help that my BMSF (Best Mom Sister Friend) was not only my best friend, she was also my best drinking buddy, but of course, as her daughter, we lived together. Therefore, I had no accountability partner, and we could work, drink, and enjoy each other daily, nonstop (of course, I was grown)! I didn't think my liquor intake was out of the norm, because everyone around me was doing it. Or so I thought?

When I was a younger adult, I would drink but not to the point of drunkenness or blacking out. I really didn't start drinking on that level until my thirties, and it slowly crept up on me. I had always been a serious person, so the more I drank, the funnier I would become, so I was told. Alcoholics run in my family's bloodline, but I would not be an alcoholic because I said so. I witnessed my family waking up in vomit, urinating on themselves, falling out all night on the front lawn, cursing, fighting, and touching people inappropriately in front of their spouse. I swore I was not going to be like other family members who had drinking problems. I was going to break this generational curse.

How can you tell a vice is slowly taking you over? Challenge time: I am not going to drink for one week. Okay, I'm not going to drink for twenty-one days. I passed the tests and then went months without drinking a drop of alcohol. I am thankful I can stop when I want to, because many individuals can't say the same. When I did drink, I would only keep small bottles of alcohol in my house; my house was a BYOB (Bring Your Own Bottle) house. I didn't realize the tricks I was playing on myself to ensure I wouldn't fall into the trap of alcoholism.

I was offered an opportunity to move from Atlanta, Georgia, to Sacramento, California. This move was one of the most eye-opening experiences of my life. It was only my daughter and I; my mother came later to watch her granddaughter as I got acclimated to California and the job. Before getting my own place in Sacramento I lived with someone for about two months. That person kept a heavily stocked bar. Well, keep in mind at my home I only kept mini bottles of my beverage of choice. Within that short time frame, I depleted the total bar almost singlehandedly. I drank every bit of liquor, and if I bought a bottle to replace that one, I drank it, too.

Now, you would think I noticed right away what was happening to me, but NO! I blamed it on the stressful move and other excuses to justify my drinking. Well, I moved out and got my own place in California. So, I was able to go back to my normal routine of monitoring the amount of alcohol kept in the house. I just want to be a social drinker and drink like a freakin' lady!

From the East Coast to the West Coast, I started hearing people say the same thing about me. You must acknowledge you've changed when your lifetime friends and new acquaintances are all saying parallel things from one coast to the other. They started telling me, "I like you better when you're not drinking; you are a great person with a wonderful, positive spirit, but when you drink you change for the worse." It was time for me to do a self-assessment and to reevaluate my drinking situation. I didn't need to look in the mirror, because my neighbor who hung out with me had secretly recorded me during one of my drinking escapades. The change in my behavior was unrecognizable and deplorable; I was appalled at myself and couldn't believe this image was me. I wasn't usually like that unless I was drinking, and that was THE problem. With time, the excessive drinking had been altering my behavior at a startling speed. I went from a social drinker to a belligerent, insulting, blackout drinker. It was so bad I couldn't remember anything when I was intoxicated. Blackouts are real. You don't know if you need to apologize to someone, how you got home . . . only to discover your car is in the driveway. Really? I drove like that, endangering myself and others? It's a startling reality that needs to be rectified, immediately!

I heard a sermon that changed my life. The sermon posed the question, why do people wait until they hit rock bottom before they seek help? See, I still felt in control over my vice because I had a job and multiple businesses, my appearance was up to par, and I had not gotten in any proven misbehaviors that warranted the police. Again, why wait until you hit rock bottom to seek help? Be proactive! It's okay to notice a vice has gotten the best of you and it is time to seek help. The very tactics I used before—I will stop drinking for a week, twenty-one days, and so on— NO LONGER WORKED! I was praying to get through the next twenty-four hours. I tried everything. My favorite libation was apple martinis or

Texas margaritas, with a triple shot of Grand Marnier. Then I switched to red wine, white wine, IPA beer, and I even tried different coolers, and back in the days, I did not count the low alcohol percent as drinking. I started understanding that my vice had gotten the best of me! My rock bottom was here.

Vices have had people drive under the influence and kill innocent people during a blackout, or get into altercations over something silly, or make fool of themselves and wake up not knowing the possible destruction they left behind. I did not want to wait to hit rock bottom. I simply did not want to lose my life or hurt someone else during one of my blackout episodes! I saw what rock bottom could do with my family, and I had heard enough stories to understand addiction was running through my veins, through my bloodline. Finally, I understood I am allergic to all alcoholic beverages, and drinking has no longer been my vice as of August 25, 2018!

I had some help along the way—thanks to everyone who helped me understand that I needed to admit my vice. You have to admit your addiction to yourself, and now I am transparently admitting it to the world. You do not have to hit rock bottom, you do not have to lose any possessions. You can take control of your truth and make some changes prior to experiencing "the worst is yet to come." Is it your time to release the vice within? Once I was able to be blatantly honest with myself and cried out for help, doors opened for me. Seeking help was one of the best decisions of my life. Again, talking, sharing, releasing the anger within will free you from your self-bondage. You'll realize the cage you've constructed has a door that's wide open, and all you need to do is step out of that prison any time you choose into a more favorable existence. It will not be easy, but it will be worth it! And YES, overcoming a vice is truly a one-day-at-a-time process, and a lifelong journey.

Even when you're free of one vice, be careful! An addictive personality means you can transfer from one addiction to another. Guess what my new vice turned into? Food! Just call me Miss Piggy, because I began to eat bad foods habitually. I had started eating like a pig. My food intake increased rapidly, and soon it was out of control. I used to be the girl who would get a salmon Caesar salad with a nice libation. But once I stopped drinking, I began to eat poorly—I would eat a hamburger, french fries, a milkshake, and still be hungry. I was trying to fill that void in yet another way. I typically don't eat beef because my body doesn't digest meat very well, but I continued to eat things I wouldn't normally eat. I had never been a sweets girl, nor a soda girl, but I started to drink soda left and right—several sodas a day, and an energy drink if I was going to be around alcohol. Then I began drinking coffee morning, noon, and night. My daughter told me, "Mom, how you are drinking nonalcoholic beverages is probably how you were drinking alcoholic beverages without noticing." Ouch! Out of the mouths of babes. In my mind, I wasn't out of control to that magnitude, but it pierced my spirit, so she may have been right.

I worked from home, and I could eat and drink as much as I wanted. Clearly, food fixation was my new addiction. Unfortunately, addictive behavior can truly transfer into a different area of your life, or you can have multiple addictions. Well, imagine eating a bag—a whole family bag—of potato chips. That's how I started to crave chocolate; white chocolate, to be exact. White chocolate filled cups, white chocolate with caramel, white chocolate with nuts and caramel, and white chocolate on almost anything were my sweets of choice. I didn't understand what was happening to me. I would have bags of them and eat them nonstop throughout the day. Of course, my body began to reflect my eating habits, from fine to fluffy, or fat. I went from 150 to 219 pounds; I'm five foot eight, so you be the judge. Have you ever had a friend or family member who has not seen you for a long time simply stare at you without ceasing? Or have you been to a reunion and people ask if such-and-such is coming, and you're literally right in front of their eyes, but they don't recognize you because you have picked up over seventy pounds? These actions work on your already fragile self-esteem. Yes, there is a dramatic difference between a size ten and a size sixteen! There is also a difference in your face, as well as your gut and your psyche. Well, I have been there, and it is not an exhilarating feeling.

No matter who notices the enormous weight gain, there is no one who notices more than yourself—especially when you're taking a shower, LOL. I must say it was truly depressing going from super-fine at one point to supersized in the same lifespan.

I weighed between 145 and 150 pounds my entire life. After giving birth, I lost my baby fat in six months. Over the years, life happened as well as age, and of course me not treating my temple as very holy, and my weight increased to 219. I felt FUGLY! When you feel that you're fat and ugly, there is no one who can persuade you that you're beautiful no matter what! In addition to my lovely weight gain, I had high blood pressure and I had to take medication to manage it. I wasn't old, but I felt and looked much older than I should at my age. Even my daughter suggested I get my swag back. My own mother said, "I was starting to look and act like Harriet Tubman. It is not an insult when you're older, but you are too young to look so stern, cold, sad, and basically, morbid!" I need to look like a MILF, not a grandma! Was my look a plea for help? Or just an outward sign of my ghosts from the past putting me on yet another path of destruction?

Switching from one vice to another was a subliminal occurrence, as well—sugar is an addictive substance. It is known to cause obesity, diabetes, and other health issues. Do you believe sugar is more addictive than drugs? Look online, remarkably interesting studies have been conducted on the effects of sugar versus drugs. I am trying to wean myself off this sugar craving. I felt like a sugar-feen, always looking for my next fix of chocolate. I didn't know what other outlet I could turn to if I said no to alcohol, no to fattening foods, and no to sugar. During this time, my body started having a reaction to removing alcohol, which is full of sugar, especially my apple martinis and Texas-style margaritas. Now my body was craving sugar in a different format, a fact unbeknownst to me until the pounds accumulated, my appearance drastically shifted, and my pride for kicking one habit had diminished.

I've spent over twenty years in the medical field, and I have worked with patients who are on dialysis. Dialysis is for patients who have kidney failure. Many of these patients have poor dietary habits. I began to study individuals who had lost a lot of weight and decided, why don't I finally take charge of my body, my holy temple, and turn a negative addiction into positive daily habits? That's what I'll do! I will change my unhealthy habits into healthy habits of positive addictions. My plan was to alter my new-found food obsession and change it to working out, eating healthy, and becoming the fittest person I could be spiritually, physically, and mentally. Now, the question was how to curb my appetite and get healthy fast. Overcoming the power of addiction versus changing to good habits would require prayer, discipline, and determination.

I started listening to great leaders and focusing on the Law of Attraction. I went on a sabbatical with very few people in my circle and focused on me. I began to change without noticing, and I documented the process I used to reprogram myself. I am so grateful and thankful that I can use my journey to do what I love doing most, which is helping people to transform their lives. My life experiences as well as my education have cultivated a passion in me that has led me to my purpose. I share my experiences to help you lean on my strength and my process of change, to help you overcome a vice that is causing more harm than good. Simply put, my vice was replaced with this purpose. And, it must be duly noted, that without conquering these vices, my purpose would have been delayed or may never have been exposed. So, the vices and the challenge to overcome them led me to a higher revelation of myself.

Alcoholism or food addiction may not be your vice. However, the transformational teachings are the same. Identify your vice and be truthful to yourself! Do you want to stop, or simply control your intake? If you said control your intake, how successful were your efforts? No one can intervene and point out to you that your vice has overtaken you. This is a journey between you, yourself, and your higher power (for me, that is God). I challenge you to look in the mirror and ask yourself: *How many seconds, minutes, hours, days, weeks, or longer can I go without indulging in my vice? Do I have to hit rock bottom? What does my rock bottom look like? How can I prevent myself from hitting rock bottom?*

Release All Within will assist with your potential to surge into your greatness.

CHAPTER 2 SELF-EVALUATION AND NOTES

1) Do you overly indulge? If so, how?

_____

_____

_____

_____

_____

_____

_____

2) Identify your vice.

_____

_____

_____

_____

_____

_____

_____

3) Do you want to stop but can't? If so, write about a time when you tried to stop.

_____

_____

_____

_____

_____

_____

_____

_____

4) Do you want help?

_____

_____

_____

_____

_____

_____

_____

_____

5) Do you have a family member, friend, or a professional person or organization that will act as your accountability partner and assist you with this process?

_____

_____

_____

_____

_____

_____

_____

_____

6) How do you imagine your life without your vice(s)?

_____

_____

_____

_____

_____

_____

_____

_____

Notes

Purge:	Get rid of unwanted feelings
Emerge:	Rise from the situation
Surge:	Propel your pain into power and purpose

Assignment: Write how you will
PURGE, EMERGE, then SURGE.

_____

_____

_____

_____

_____

_____

_____

_____

_____

_____

_____

_____

_____

Addiction Hotline:

855-315-4766

National Eating Disorders Association:

800-931-2237

CHAPTER 3
SUICIDAL SOCIETY

Have you ever thought it would be easier to go to sleep and never wake up? Is your life mundane, repetitive, or simply missing a spark? Do you feel overwhelmed, underachieved, unappreciated, or merely like a failure? What about financial issues—debts, taxes, loans, bills, money, money, money? Are you too rich, too poor, too broke to pay attention? What about relationship problems? Do you feel like a people pleaser—you get bullied, can't stand up for yourself? Do you feel judged, depressed, and ready to call it quits? If you committed suicide and ended your life too soon, you would never know the finished product!

Have you ever woken up and thought, ENOUGH! I had enough. I began to reflect on my life. All the failed dreams, failed relationships, failed success . . . Who was I comparing my life to? Well, I've felt defeated a few times in life, and I thought quitting would be easier than continuing this fight. I am so thankful I had a loving team to pour into me and encourage me by telling me how much I meant to them. They reminded me of my purpose, gifts, and talents, and simply encouraged me to keep on fighting until I win! Thank God I had a tribe, because there are many who do not, and they have to either create their tribe or learn to encourage themselves. This is difficult, but not impossible. I'm possible!

Actors, actresses, models, celebrities; the mega wealthy, rich, poor; each ethnicity, each gender; any age, young, middle-aged, and older, the list goes on and on—suicide does not discriminate. I realize some people do not have family or friends to help them overcome this feeling of defeat. Some people are surrounded by people but still feel isolated. I am your new friend by faith who will pray for you to see the value in your life! This chapter is a guide to help you identify and evaluate the pain that has caused you to want to commit suicide. Before anything else, you will need to seek professional assistance! **(If you are having thoughts that you would be better off dead than alive, call someone before your thoughts become a reality. Here is the Suicide and Crisis Lifeline. Reach out to them immediately by dialing 988.)**

The first time I noticed I was having suicidal idea-tions was in elementary school. As a child, I was dif-ferent. I was born broken; I always felt a sense of rejection. My mother and family loved me deeply, but I never quite fit in. My mother was the beautiful swan, and I was the ugly duckling. Yes, when I was younger, I felt like I was the ugly duckling of the fam-ily because my mother was not only beautiful on the outside, she was the complete package. She was a lot to measure up against. I didn't just feel like an ugly duckling, some of the kids called me that at school. I grew up in an era where enhancements such as fake hair, lashes, or any additives to help young ladies look extraordinary did not exist. Kids at school could be very cruel, especially when you were the teacher's pet. I was always asked to assist the teacher, including telling on students when they misbehaved, and I did so with pride just to get even with them for hurting my feelings daily.

One day three boys ganged up on me, not knowing my uncles taught me how to fight. I punched one boy so hard that I gave him a black eye and the other two boys ran off. After that, someone wanted to fight me every day to see if I was a better fighter than them.

I'm glad social media didn't exist when I was younger. I asked my mother if I could move to a different school because these kids were bullying me. But it was as if every school I went to, they heard the story of the fight and the new school's best fighter wanted to fight me; no matter where I went, I couldn't escape. I simply wanted to go to school and be left alone (secretly, I would have enjoyed being accepted and relished but that never happened).

Over the years, I went to over five different schools, not including vocational trade schools and colleges. My entire childhood, from elementary school, middle school, high school, and trade school . . . I fought! I laugh as I write this because I am still fighting, just not with my fists. Now I fight to survive the lemons tossed in my direction. Just as I did back then, I need to learn how to surpass all obstacles by turning those lemons into delicious lemonade. The only tool in my toolbox was avoidance, to run away, which of course wasn't an effective way to live, nor the best way to make successful decisions and advance. But it was all I knew.

As a child, when you have people wanting to fight

you daily, your grades will suffer, and I was the only child. I had a few friends at school, but something was missing. I became full of rage and secretly wanted to hurt the kids being mean to me. Instead of hurting them, I realized, I could just hurt myself. Yes, that's what I would do. As I was taking a bath, I had a razor and a knife because I did not know which one worked faster. I took the razor and I cut just the first layer of skin. It hurt so badly it was like a mother giving birth; blood was squirting out and I was crying and in pain just from the small slit. I was scared. I wrapped my wrist, and I did not go through with it. I want to thank God for understanding my intense pain and loving me through it, because otherwise I would not be here today!

If I had died young, I would never have had the opportunity to find my true purpose and walk in it. Pouring into others and helping them see themselves as their elevated self is a gift that has made my journey worth surviving. Do you know what you would be missing out on if you cut your life short? What footprint are you destined to leave in this world? What mark are you to imprint to show that you lived and made a difference?

IS SUICIDE THE CHOICE BETWEEN LIFE AND DEATH?

BLEEDING OUT

I would like to share a story about the crossroad between living and giving into death. This story is slightly graphic due to a medical condition I was experiencing. If you are sensitive to such content, you may want to skip this story. I was hemorrhaging, bleeding from my rectum off and on for over two weeks. I did not tell anyone, because I felt like my life had become repetitive and I felt hopeless. I was worth more dead than alive—if I bled out, my daughter would have more than enough money to go to college and start her life as a successful entrepreneur. I LOVE my daughter, mother, and family, but I was only existing and not living a purposeful life. I was disappointed with myself for not being as successful as I had planned.

I had recently relocated from California, maintaining a position as a rep working both the northern and southern territories, and returned to Atlanta to take a position that would allow me to focus on parenthood and not the money. I thought this job was a blessing in disguise because I could focus on motherhood and not do so much traveling. I was one of the first hired to open another outpatient medical facility with the certainty that I would become their marketing/sales rep. When I spoke with the manager, they knew my ultimate goal was to become part of their team. However, the manager I had established a rapport with was asked to resign. The old manager returned, and he resembled a young version of Donald Trump but taller. I told him of my interest in the position, and he had the audacity to tell me not now, nor ever would I be the right fit for their sales/marketing team (after I had tremendously increased their net worth with my marketing strategies and effort). Ouch!

I had been working and getting paid half my previous salary with the assurance I would get this promotion. Not now, not ever—that comment sucked the air out of me! I was an excellent employee, arrived early, stayed late, received excellent reviews from my manager, and the patients loved me! I had so many positive patient surveys/comments that I received multiple bonuses. However, his piercing comment kept playing in my head, so much so that it made me instantly numb. I struggled to hold back my tears standing right there in his face and I don't even remember if I was successful.

My life was a routine—wake up at three, get to work by five thirty, work my ass off, pick up my child, and guess what? Ding, ding, ding! Hit the alarm clock going off to recycle the same mundane day after day for over two and a half years. My zeal left my spirit. Not now, not ever . . . Why was I working for this company? You can give your absolute best and it's still not enough. Did I want to live or die?

The hemorrhaging was getting worse. Blood was filling up the toilet and I was preparing myself for death. I made sure my life policy was up to par and my affairs were in order to ensure everyone was taken care of financially without leaving a burden on my family. I remember some of my family members not preparing properly by purchasing life insurance, which is very inexpensive, but it's extremely expensive to bury someone without it. We all live and we will all die, just at various times.

At this time, I was feeling weak. My eyes had dark

circles underneath, and my face looked pale and life-less. It was time to finally tell my mother what was going on. Her eyes began to fill with tears and she told me hell no, absolutely not! She said she needed my love to exist and she needed me to continue to be the supreme daughter to her, the exceptional mother to my daughter, and informed me that I had to fulfill God's plan for my life. She told me, "Do not quit and give into the enemy's ploy! That one man and any similar situation should not be allowed to govern over you and determine your fate. No one should EVER possess that kind of power over you, regard-less of the circumstance. Quitting is easier than fighting."

I told her of my failed dreams, my job situation, how I had no love life while everyone around me was getting married. Overall, my looks, mind, body, and spirit weren't at the highest vibration. After explain-ing all this to my mother, I told her I would pray on it. Always rest before making a decision, because joy usually comes in the morning.

Although this is not a typical suicidal story, I had a choice like you have a choice. Do you want to live, or die by bleeding out, or commit suicide? I woke up the next morning and decided I wanted to fight for my life! I was not one to call out sick, but I called out sick and went to the gastroenterologist to find out what was wrong with me. They gave me an emergency procedure and it rectified my situation instantly (both literally and figuratively).

One visit to the right specialist saved my life. After that life-or-death situation, I now had to make a choice. Do I continue to live the life I was ready to die to escape, or do I reevaluate and make changes toward what makes me joyful and what makes life worth living? What are my dreams, purpose, and passion? I had been given another chance. I was reborn, and the blood I had shed was rebuilding my new wineskin by extracting the past failures, pains, and stagnation. It was time to redefine what was important to my existence. Living a purposeful life is not a job, it is maximizing all natural gifts, talents, and selfless behavior to fulfill your calling. Helping others elevate themselves is something I have always done naturally, and it is part of my legacy, my DNA, and my destiny. At that moment I made the conscientious decision to fight the good fight! That man and his statement had fueled me to give those opposite of what I received. The lemons, once again, had inspired me to seek and deliver the kindness that humanity so desperately needs along with the secret steps to achieving such.

Asking why I went through certain tests is simply to edify my testimony. Seeking the message out of my mess taught me how to identify with soldiers who have survived the victory of war. There's a cost to knocking down the barriers to transform into our higher selves but, in the end, it provides dividends and an internal illumination for the world to behold and enjoy. It promises a zeal for life that surpasses the desire for solely a salary, the need for validation, or being beholden to one person's words or actions. All this began to unfold as I declared my renewed life and took charge of my own destiny.

In order to change, you must be honest with yourself. Do you want to live? If so, what is your why? Why has your life been spared? If even young people are dying from natural causes, yet we are still on earth, why have our lives been spared? We must have a purpose that has not been fulfilled! Do not give up before your story unfolds. You have the ability and the authority to write your very own chapters—and guess what? You are the author, the main character, and the star! How awesome is that?

We all have a legacy, a purpose, a talent that lies within all mankind. Only you know your burning desire; do not let a setback put you six feet under before you can fulfill your destiny. Go outside and take a deep breath—inhale, hold, exhale, and release temporary pain. Most situations or circumstances are temporary. Suicide is permanent! And if your pain is permanent, again, why are you still here? Don't be too proud to get professional help or get into group sessions with those walking through similar pains. Direct communication with therapists as well as group therapy have proven to be amazing tools that I now have in my toolbox. And occasionally I go back to them, whenever I need to. Also, stop comparing yourself to anyone else. There's only one unique you, and you have the wand to live and create your world according to your own standards, no one else's. Lastly, stop looking and living in the past, it's gone. Practice living in the NOW. Steer away from putting too much thought into the future. You must retrain your brain and thought processes, daily, until NOW thoughts are a standard routine. Take hold of each of those stinking repetitive narratives in your mind and list them if you must. When they arise—and they will because you have given them years of permission— take immediate hold of each and every one of these thoughts. Evaluate the validity and turn it around toward the positive. For example, "You're an ugly duckling," as the kids said in my youth, but I stopped that now, by saying that was then and this is now. I've been a model and received many compliments on my outward appearance. So, bless those who said negative things about me light years ago. Pay less attention to what people think of you and care more about what you think of yourself! Possess each of your thoughts and begin to control them, rather than them controlling you. Otherwise, it can put you right back in the dark, lonely, and frightening rabbit hole of depression and hopelessness. You can begin this change of your life today! What is causing you to feel like ending your life? Let's help you purge your past, emerge into your present, then surge into your wholeness!

If you're having suicidal thoughts, use the A.S.K. Approach:

Acknowledge the truth. If you or your loved ones see a sign of depression, act on it.

Seek help for yourself or your loved one IMMEDIATELY.

Know time is of the essence; a thought can turn into an action.

Suicidal Hotline Services: 800-273-8255 (TALK)

HOW TO OVERCOME SUICIDAL BEHAVIOR

➤ Take a shortcut from my journey to get some immediate results. Because honestly, it may take a long time for you to become your best, most amazing person, but it only takes seconds, one word, that can elevate the way you see yourself and how others see you. Yes, as a man or woman thinketh, they can become, but it takes work! Practice by capturing your every thought, and then recondition your thoughts, one thought at a time. Remember to let go of comparative thinking, dwelling on the past, and putting too much thought toward the future. Focus on positive and solution-oriented thoughts. At first, it is difficult to captivate and re-condition the mind, but eventually a lot of these thoughts cease to exist and you have more mental space for your intrinsic creativity, positivity, and self-love. This will also promote positive mind imagery that then can manifest into your reality.

➤ Seek help! A well-matched therapist can be a key player to unveiling concealed emotions and their origin, to extract what is true and what has been magnified, only in your own mind, which doesn't necessarily bear truth on reality but formulates the repetitive tape recording in your mind.

➤ Be selective and protective of the people in your inner circle. Allow only those who can weather your endeavors and avoid those who drink from your well and never replenish it.

➢ Organize your thoughts and begin to consistently journal. Reflect on your journal to document your incremental growth and every so often go back and read your early entries as a compass to your intentional positive changes.

➢ Establish goals pertinent to your weak areas. Make your goals baby steps that are attainable and assign a projected date of completion for each goal. Celebrate when the goal has been mastered. Then, undertake a new one.

➢ Develop a kinship with a like-minded person who is also putting forth effort to grow. Be each other's nonjudgmental cheerleaders. Engage in reciprocal dialogue to discuss your progress and share different effective tools. Let this be someone you can laugh or cry with; it may even be your spouse.

➤ If you are spiritual, sharpen your relationship with the Creator and feel the agape love that man cannot give and relish in it.

➤ Spoil yourself daily. You are worth it! The bubble bath, the nap, reading a juicy novel, jogging, eating that slice of chocolate cake—whatever feeds your spirit, work it into your daily schedule and take that time to stroke your own heart.

➤ Take your vitamins and pre-scribed medication, eat regular healthy meals, exercise your mind and body, and lastly, get enough sleep.

➤ Volunteer! To get out of yourself, volunteer and serve with an organization of your liking. It brings so much joy and pride when you help someone else. It also helps to fill a void that an unhealthy vice is currently feeling.

➤ There is a formula for a healthy

and sound life, to a degree, but we must take the necessary steps of planning, implementing, and replacing our old habits with a fresh set of standards of life to optimize your wholesome "you."

CHAPTER 3 SELF-EVALUATION AND NOTES

1) Do you think your life is repetitive? If so, how?

_____

_____

_____

_____

_____

_____

_____

2) Do you want to live or die? If so, why?

_____

_____

_____

_____

_____

_____

_____

3) Do you take medication? Do any of them promote suicidal behavior?

_____

_____

_____

_____

_____

_____

_____

4) Do you know what makes you happy? If so, what or who makes you happy and why? How can you fit this person or activity more into your schedule?

_____

_____

_____

_____

_____

_____

_____

5) Do you know what your purpose is? If so, what is it? Are you living in your purpose? What steps can you take?

_____

_____

_____

_____

_____

_____

_____

Notes

_____

_____

_____

_____

_____

_____

_____

Purge:	Get rid of unwanted feelings
Emerge:	Rise from the situation
Surge:	Propel your pain into power and purpose

Assignment: Write how you will
PURGE, EMERGE, then SURGE.

National Suicide Prevention Hotline:

800-273-8255 (TALK)

CHAPTER 4
CHURCH CRISES

This chapter is to help you identify the broken parts within you that contain matters deeper than the physical. It should be your goal to dig deep so you can identify what is holding you back from rising to your next level, mentally, physically, and spiritually! Many of us may have been hurt, betrayed, or shocked by surprising behaviors in a church setting. (If you have not experienced "church crises," you can replace this chapter's title with "Overcoming Betrayal.") As you read this chapter, you'll notice I did not include a denomination, because church crises are simply to assist anyone who went to a place of fellowship under the pretense they were entering a place of peace, truth, and supernatural rejuvenation, and left feeling betrayed. If you've experienced this, you may have felt confused, disappointed, or deceived by the words, deeds, or actions of these "spiritually kind" people!

Keep in mind a man or woman of God is simply a

human being. Many of those with titles such as bishop, pastor, priest, reverend, deacon, church server, staff, and all who represent a steward over the house of God are simply flesh. They bleed, sin, and fall short just like you and I; they are just a man or woman of God, they are not God, and they are not made without blemishes, flaws, or imperfections! People in the church can cause pain that hurts so bad it changes your views on religion and possibly God. My journey to this understanding took over two decades to unveil, overcome, and heal from, so feel free to take a shortcut by identifying your personal pain more quickly than I did.

My mother raised me in the church. She worked at a church and truly followed all the traditions, and even though she was a cussing Christian, she was a woman of integrity. The first church I went to, the pastor was caught sleeping with a lot of young girls and getting them pregnant. It was shameful how the church ignored these ungodly activities; you'd think that's how a man of the cloth normally behaves. It was easy back then to keep church secrets, family secrets, and individual secrets because social media did not exist, and no one had a voice unless you were someone of valor. I wish social media had been out back in those days; that pedophile along with many other church leaders would have been jailed. Honestly, I was young, and I truly didn't process this behavior until later, much later.

The next church I went to, the pastor was also sleeping with a lot of the young ladies of the church and getting them pregnant. Once I got older and realized what was happening, I viewed church as no more than a social gathering to play with the kids and learn a few scriptures. In my era, we didn't have a choice; it was embedded in us every Sunday that church was mandated, no matter what you did the night before. Later, I noticed a shift in my mother as far as church was concerned. My mother had always been a cussing and fun Christian, but she was seeking God with her whole heart on another level, and she started to serve more at the church. It was as if she believed the more she served, the more she could show God how much she loved Him. In truth, the more she served, the more she heard about what went on behind closed doors. She warned me to be careful when I got older and served in the church, because when you learn the secrets of a church it can scar you and your relationship with God. Over the years, her words continued to resonate in my spirit, and I learned she was right.

After becoming a "grown" adult, I decided to seek a church of my own. My auntie invited me to her church, the New Birth Missionary Baptist Church. I attended the church when it was small, quaint, and still packed to capacity at several services. The choir, music, theatrics, and passion behind his message brought his sermon to life. Later, his church grew into a megachurch; literally, I watched the change from the ground up. I learned so much from the bishop. He was extremely anointed and taught me the word as he knew it to be. I will not discredit him. He grew me up from a babe in Christ to a young adult of Christ. I got baptized and honestly planned on staying with that church forever, because it felt like home to me when it was small. When I moved to Marietta, I continued to drive almost an hour to church every Sunday without hesitation. I remember growing leaps and bounds listening to the word. He encouraged us to be faithful tithers and he had us serve the community. I witnessed the bishop give to the less fortunate and elevate those who were broken. When

I gave birth to my daughter, she was christened there; her name is Genesis.

As everything at New Birth began to change, I noticed a disconnect. The church had already become an ultra-megachurch that was constantly expanding, and the larger the services grew, the more I noticed a change in the bishop. It was slow but visible. When the church had been smaller, we would hug him, and he was simply present and approachable. But as the church grew, he began to preach about his "ego" and that is exactly what was happening—his ego was expanding. He would always tell us to study the word for ourselves. That kept resonating within my spirit.

As a consistent tither and a constant servant in the church, I was disappointed when I lost my job and had to ask the church for financial help. I was going through a crisis, but I was declined because I didn't meet certain criteria. After ten years, from 1997 to 2007, I felt the need to take a break from New Birth and all churches. I took the bishop's advice, and I began to seek God with my whole heart and read the entire Bible and studied for myself. I am forever grateful that he taught us to study for ourselves and find our own relationship with God. He told us that because man is flesh and no man is perfect, mankind will disappoint you every time.

After a two-year hiatus, my daughter climbed on my lap and said, "Mommy, we need to go back to church." I told her to find us a church and she did. I wanted her to seek God from her own mindset, not mine. I went to church with a new outlook—to hear the word, find fellowship, serve, and be a cheerful tither. As I was with the previous church, I saw the same megachurch syndrome occur. The pastor was approachable, loving, humble and helped the unchurched. But once he moved from a small church to a large church, the same changes occurred. I served and tithed faithfully, and my daughter loved the church she had picked out.

One day my car broke down; it was no big deal because I had enough in my savings to get it fixed, two thousand dollars, but it would wipe me out. The church used to be close, about eight miles, but the new megachurch was far away, approximately twenty miles. I worked an estimated fifteen miles away in Sandy Springs and traveled this distance on the weekdays to serve. I began to serve more than worship. I am, or was, a giver who couldn't say no. I have since adopted the mindset that NO is a full sentence and I now say no before yes. If rushed, I've got to check in with my Holy Spirit before I move. Well, here came testing the spirit with the spirit. I was linked to an email thread, and they would always ask us to help on this thread. Well, my car broke down again and I hadn't had a chance to restock my savings from the first hit. I asked everyone on the email thread to please give my daughter and me a ride to church. Unfortunately, rideshare services didn't exist during this time, just expensive taxicabs. I asked again. At this point I had served, I believe, for two years on several committees. I had been a faithful member, and I even got rebaptized at this church. So when I said, "WILL ANYONE GIVE ME A RIDE TO CHURCH? HELLO? SOS?" Nope—flatline, crickets! No one checked on me. It was as if no one cared. Yep, this was painful. And honestly, I was done!

When the truth had been revealed about my pastor(s), I was too young and naive. I didn't want an imperfect man pouring into my spirit. I now realize a pastor is simply an imperfect man blessed with a godly anointing to spread the word. Leaders who misuse this gift for monetary reasons, sexual acts, control, or other demonic reasons will not be judged by man, but the God who blessed them with these gifts. I also learned a valuable lesson over the years. I realized that when tragedies knocked me down and I needed assistance from my church, no one was there for me—I was denied support for various reasons that did not make sense. Yet, God still provided! He always had a ram in the bush and his help would oftentimes come from an unexpected source.

My traditional way of thinking has completely changed as far as church is concerned. I am no theologian; your spiritual journey is between you and God. I don't even know where I will be spiritually by the time you read this book, because when you have a connection with God, he will direct your path, purpose, and plans!

Not every leader is corrupt. Bishop Patrick Ivey, thank you for providing food to my daughter and I during that time I lost my job and when our refrigerator was empty!

Thank you, leaders who have maintained your integrity, and to the many godly ministers who are leading their members according to the teachings of God. I know the flesh is weak and it is hard to maintain a high level of decorum while your every move is being scrutinized. And yet some of you truly do your best to conform to biblical laws, and for that, I am grateful!

To those of you who lost faith because of what was done to you in church, I can truly identify with your pain. Don't let this hold you back from your purpose! The first step is being honest about your feelings. Go to a quiet place and have a talk with God. If you're mad at God, be real because he knows your heart. Talk to someone and start sharing your story so you can start healing. There are church crises hotlines that can help. Just remember flesh is not the same as spirit.

Turn your pain into a purpose that you're passionate about and watch a new plan unfold for your life. I am a living witness! But be patient with yourself, because you will need to walk through the process, including applying forgiveness to all parties involved, including yourself.

CHAPTER 4 SELF-EVALUATION AND NOTES

1) Do you attend a church or a place where you thought you could trust its leaders?

_____

_____

_____

_____

_____

_____

_____

2) Have you experienced any physical, emotional, or spiritual damage at this place? If so, how?

_____

_____

_____

_____

_____

_____

_____

3) Do you still attend the place that betrayed your trust? If so, have you spoken to someone about it? What was the outcome? If not, why haven't you, and how are you dealing with the betrayal? Is this church a stopping place?

_____

_____

_____

_____

_____

_____

_____

4) Do you know God for yourself and do you blame God for this situation?

_____

_____

_____

_____

_____

_____

5) Write down a list of people who have hurt you. Have you forgiven them? Now, list the people you have hurt and asked for forgiveness.

Notes

Purge:	Get rid of unwanted feelings
Emerge:	Rise from the situation
Surge:	Propel your pain into power and purpose

Assignment: Write how you will
PURGE, EMERGE, then SURGE.

Church Crises Hotline Services: 1-800-276-1562

Report a bishop at https://reportbishopabuse.org/

CHAPTER 5
WORK WARS

Do you love your job? If you love your job or your business, this chapter is not for you! Do you enjoy the way you're earning an income? This chapter is for people who dislike their job. Do you have any reasons you despise going to work? Do you feel overworked? Do you feel undervalued? Are you underpaid with an excessive workload? Do you dislike your boss or coworkers? Do you simply hate going into the office? Are you finding reasons to force yourself to go to work, or always conjuring excuses to stay home? Work Wars is designed to help you identify what is causing your war at work so you can elevate yourself to your purpose.

A work war is the war within your workplace that causes an uneasy work environment. Over the years, I have experienced each of the work wars listed above, but there is one that has taunted me on each job. Before telling you the one that haunted me from job to job, I will share how I overcame my work wars.

If you have choices, DO NOT TAKE a peon position expecting a boss outcome. Typically the position you are hired for is how management views you. For example, if you are typically a manager, do not take a receptionist position in hopes of being recognized and promoted to manager. Oftentimes, you will be overlooked. Before experiencing this lesson, I was under the impression that if I demonstrated my skill set, which consisted of sales, marketing, administration, and managerial skills, plus over twenty years of medical experience (typically a six-figure position), I would move up in the company at an accelerated pace.

NOT the case! I took a job I was overqualified for, and I assumed I would be promoted and eventually paid my worth to match my skills in a short time frame, as long as I demonstrated excellent work ethic. Out of all the accolades I received—patient satisfaction surveys, managers complimenting my professionalism and high level of knowledge and work ethic—I learned a lesson. Seek a job that meets your desired salary to cover all your expenses, such as your mortgage, utilities, car note, all bills, because your pay raise will never increase enough to cover your current lifestyle if you take a peon position. Most importantly, the company will rarely view you as anything but that "peon" and will pimp you for all you have. You're trying to prove yourself while they're simply raping your mind and stamping their name on your phenomenal recommendations.

Does your work war include a salaried position? Being salaried has its perks and disadvantages. Many times, salaried jobs are designed for the employer to complete job tasks without focusing on the number of hours it will take to complete the assignment. Typically, these positions exceed the typical forty-hour, seven-days-a-week work schedule. The perk is knowing the dollar amount per check and the exact pay date. Upon hire, try to negotiate with the hiring employer. For example, request every other Friday off, if possible, or negotiate a perk for yourself so you don't feel underpaid and/or undervalued.

My work war typically involves the people in the organization. People have a tendency to change in a negative way at each job site. I understand the rule of thumb that when you are the common dominator, then you must be the problem. Well, life lessons, growth, and pain sometimes must be repeated for you to understand your plan might need to change! Perhaps a conventional corporate job was never meant to be your end-all career position and you are continuing to try to fit a square peg in a round hole. That was me (it just took me multiple jobs to discover this).

A new job, new rules, and new people. Have you ever noticed the job is normally manageable, in some cases incredible, if you're doing what you enjoy? It is the people you work with who can make or break your work experience. As the new kid on the block, I am old enough to know that alliances of substantial time already exist.

You have the social butterflies who hang out together, and the loners who make it known they do not want to interact simply by their nonresponsive demeanor. Others smile, nod their head as a form of communication, or are kind to everyone, but keep conversation to a minimum. You have the gossips who take the information you tell them and add or subtract to your story, usually making you look like the bad guy. Of course there will also be the "shit starter," who always starts shit and then says they don't know how this shit got started.

Last but not least we have the deadliest of them all! These people seem like they're part of the team, but do their Evil Knievel deeds alone. They are the masterminds of destruction, puppeteers, and yet they always seem to receive positive accolades. These are the ones who claim to be holier than thou but are really Satan in disguise. They don't just want to hurt you, but destroy your good name. Somehow these evil people seem to never get caught. I call this type of person the slithering snake. This slithering snake has followed me from job to job, and I never realized it until I watched a movie called *Fallen,* with Denzel Washington. This movie helped me to understand how Satan works, especially the slithering snakes. I began to understand how the snake was following me from job to job.

This snake will smile in your face while plotting to bite you with its venomous fangs. Day by day it wraps its long tail around you, not only to bite you but to suck the very life out of you until you quit, have medical issues from stress, or go insane. This slithering snake spreads lies and creates stories slandering your name. The snake uses its powers to persuade coworkers who previously befriended you to suddenly dislike you. Again, I have worked in the medical field for over twenty years, which is a long time to subject myself to this abuse, only to discover my work war pattern: the slithering snake constantly followed me everywhere I went in that industry.

While reflecting on this chapter, I realized something. I must be transparent with you so you can see that my pain from my jobs ultimately pushed me into my purpose. I had to be honest with myself and analyze each situation since the common denominator was me.

Each job started off amazing! I would learn the job and typically exceed the company's expectations. However, that was never enough. I was either forced to resign or was fired from each job, thus pushing me into my purpose. I didn't realize that until I heard that billionaire Mark Cuban became a successful entrepreneur, a mogul on *Shark Tank*, and owner of the Mavericks after quitting or being fired from three straight jobs. Also, Walt Disney created Disney World after he was fired from his job at the *Kansas City Star* for lack of imagination. Therefore, if your work wars are ongoing, you may need to reflect, speak to a life coach, or ask someone of influence to assist you in finding a purposeful path.

The purpose that has been burning deep in my soul, maybe ever since I was born, is to help the downtrodden. Because of all of my trials and defeats, I can help others with insight and without judgement. These people can come in many forms: the homeless, the hopeless, the sick, the elderly, etc. My passion metamorphosed into specifically having the desire to initially help people like me. Basic good, law-abiding, intelligent, and compassionate people who are hurting and don't know how to address all of these issues. I wanted to share my story so that perhaps you could take a shortcut in life and come to some profound conclusions faster, earlier, and with less heartache than I have had to endure. Walking in this passion gives me an ultimate sense of pride and accomplishment that a nine-to-five could never do. By doing the Creator's will and embellishing my God-given talents to reach one and teach one is the fulfillment that my total being has been longing for.

CHAPTER 5 SELF-EVALUATION AND NOTES

1) Are you a good fit for your place of employment? How so?

_____

_____

_____

_____

_____

_____

_____

2) Are you personally fulfilled with your work life? Explain.

_____

_____

_____

_____

_____

_____

_____

_____

3) Do you want more out of your career? List some examples of your goals.

_____

_____

_____

_____

_____

_____

_____

4) Do you have multiple streams of income? List all current and future ones.

_____

_____

_____

_____

_____

_____

_____

5) Write out your daily routine. Do you maximize your twenty-four hours in a day, or do you need to make changes? How happy do you feel on a daily basis?

_____

_____

_____

_____

_____

_____

_____

Notes

_____

_____

_____

_____

_____

_____

_____

Purge: Get rid of unwanted feelings

Emerge: Rise from the situation

Surge: Propel your pain into power and
              purpose

Assignment: Write how you will
PURGE, EMERGE, then SURGE.

NATASHAY STARR

EEOC Equal Employment Opportunity

Commission: 877-497-5866

CHAPTER 6
RACISM EXISTS

Racism is a touchy subject, but we need to address this painful topic to review and release our anger. We must agree that racism is far greater than a divide over Ebony and Ivory skin tones. We have divisions within different countries, religions, economic statuses, sexual preferences, or overall appearance such as attire, tattoos, piercings, hairstyles, and any other visible nontraditional uniqueness. As you read this chapter, be truthful to yourself of ways you may have felt overlooked because you did not fit into a status quo, or any time you alienated another because of one of these dispositions.

Racism makes a person uncomfortable and ill at ease, all the time. Every day is like an ongoing training to keep your guard up moment to moment, which is your defense mechanism (and can cause high blood pressure, obesity, anxiety disorders, etc.). Have you ever had a person treat you as if you were invisible?

You're right there with the group, but all you verbalize is ignored. Or you walk up to a group of cohorts, and they turn their bodies to let you know you are unwelcome. How about when you're in meetings and your grandiose suggestions are belittled, but in several months, they've implemented your suggestion, yet you receive no accolades? And then people "forget" where that suggestion originated. The examples could go on endlessly.

Ouch! This is a topic people shy away from! It is not a light subject; however, the picture will be painted with dull colors for you to identify what racial or discriminatory damage has been done to you. In order to elevate yourself to the next level, you must identify some of the racist or discriminatory behaviors that have happened to you. Why is this important? You will run into the same type of person within your career; therefore you must address the issue now, calmly and with decorum! You don't want to explode and lash out, especially with today's social media because that pent-up frustration can cost you everything you've worked so hard to gain.

If you're in a community that has made you feel

ostracized for being you, it's time to change your surroundings. Find people of like minds and create your tribe that makes you feel proud to be yourself. If you notice, most people hang with others they are comfortable with, people of like minds. Do you typically socialize with people based on whether they're upper class, lower class, religious, nonreligious, straight, LGBTQIA (lesbian, gay, bisexual, transgender, queer, intersex, asexual/agender), blue collar, white collar, a certain political affiliation, sports fanatics, or connoisseurs, or whether they share your fetishes or belong to similar recovering groups? Racism exists, everywhere.

What group of people makes you shine like a diamond? Do you shun those who do not fit into your group or treat them differently? Search within and see how you can release your hatred and/or internal biases. Most of us carry these learned or ascertained traits either consciously or subconsciously. What can you do, today, to embrace and invite a "different" type of person into your personal space? How can you practice the necessary manners and ask the introductory questions to learn who that person is and discover what you two may have in common?

"I can't breathe!" These are the words uttered in 2020 by George Floyd, one of *many* Ebony men killed by a careless police officer. Can you believe today that racism still exists? When I was part of a team who researched unfortunate and unsettling Black deaths, we researched specifically the death of Kendrick Johnson, for which we created a documentary. People need to be careful listening to the media, because often we are buying into lies about sudden unresolved deaths. Some cities have never convicted an Ivory person for killing an Ebony person. The power of media is often used to manipulate our minds into believing what they tell us is the gospel truth while instead they're sweeping important truths and empirical evidence under the rug. Keep in mind people in power may very well be racist. They can misuse and abuse their authority and have the world love or hate you, simply by showing visuals and focusing on key words that sensationalize and appeal to the emotions of the self-proclaimed superior race. Needless to say, because of certain discoveries and threats, we had to cancel the scheduled documentary viewing as planned. The team had a passion for assisting families with controversial and unresolved cases and helping to bring them closure. Rest in peace to all who have died prematurely from racial hate crimes. This song is for you: "It's Unfortunate." However, thanks to this era we have smartphones that can record the irrevocable truth, but not even this visual ensures that justice will prevail. This demonstrates how racism runs through the veins of almost every bureaucracy and how its strength can override evident breaches of our rights: "we hold these truths to be self-evident that all men are created equal," as part of the US Declaration of Independence of 1776, almost 250 years ago.

Over the years, I've noticed racism was covert, covered in silence, but in recent years it has become overt—open, obvious, and unapologetic. It felt like racism had subsided, but over recent years more people have displayed hatred toward any group of people who is different from them. Racism exists, and it hurts to the degree that it penetrates the soul and causes deep depression that continues to compound each and every day of a person's life. Carrying this appendage around daily adds stress to the emotions of the heart and its functions, inflates cortisol levels, and contributes to other physical, emotional, and psychological factors that keep one off balance, just from living in a judgmental world.

I grew up in an era where Dr. Martin Luther King Jr.'s teachings were extremely prevalent. His "I Have a Dream" speech empowered all of us to believe that one day we would be able to hold hands with different ethnicities, which implied unity and individual judgement would overcome whole-group stereotypes. See, 1865 is the year slavery ended on paper, but racism still persists. Racism is deeper than the pigment of one's skin. As a Black woman with Sisterlocs (research natural hair/Sisterlocs) who has been fortunate enough to live in Atlanta, Iowa, London, Germany, and California, and be very well traveled, I will tell you, racism is found everywhere. I personally have experienced racism both traditional and nontraditional, and unfortunately, it's so much more apparent in the US compared to abroad.

As a child, I was not familiar with racism until I had my first real experience of traditional racism. When I was in elementary school, my best friend and I were nicknamed Oreo cookies. She was a beautiful Ivory female and of course I am a beautiful Ebony queen. One day my white BFF was having a massive birthday party. She invited almost everyone from our school to her amazing birthday party. The kids started to talk about what they were going to wear and how they were going to do their hair. This birthday party was supposed to be the highlight of the entire year. Her family was financially set, so money was not an issue. Pony rides, bouncy houses, slip-n-slides, cotton candy machines, popcorn machines, face painters, just the whole nine yards. However, I wasn't invited because of the color of my skin, per her parents' directive. People have haters everywhere for every reason, so make your haters your motivators (which is easy to say)! Racism is a deep form of hate, and it is as abundant as the air we breathe. People judge and discriminate for many reasons. This racism subliminally creates anger, depression, and/or a constant weight on the victim, which keeps the victim tense and constantly on alert.

Because I automatically assumed my bestie was going to invite me to her birthday party, I never even thought to ask. I assumed without question I was going to the party. I bought a new outfit, and my hair was styled to perfection. I asked Oreo if she wanted me to come early to help set up the birthday decorations. She looked at me as if she wanted to cry and she said, "You know you are my bestie, but you are not invited." Lol! I thought she was joking, so I laughed and laughed but she never joined in. I asked her, "Are you serious?" She said, "Yes, I am as serious as a heart attack." She began to explain. I'm not sure if my hearing was up to par, but she asked me if I had heard of the KKK. Duh, of course, who hasn't? The KKK used to walk down my street fully dressed in their all-white attire and regalia. Their garments looked like white sheets with a pointed hat and two holes cut out for only their eyes to be exposed. They walked down our street in Stone Mountain, Georgia, Main Street subdivision to be exact, and they made it very clear how much they hated Blacks moving into their neighborhood. She said, "My dad is the head of the KKK, and if you come to my home, they may LYNCH you!" That was my very first encounter with racial discrimination, but it was far from my last.

As an adult, my hair, Sisterlocs, has either been embraced by those who like natural hair, or I have been negatively judged by the corporate powers that be. People will automatically make assumptions when I wear my natural hair, and thus, new stereo-types are birthed using the old methodologies. The subliminal, unwritten-but-well-understood preju-dices of these massive entities that govern America and its workforce and people prevail.

One example of a stereotypical question I receive (because of my hairdo, mind you) is: Do you smoke weed? NO, I do not do ANY drugs. Some naturalistic individuals do smoke, but do not assume all natural-ists smoke weed because they, emphatically, do not. Do you hear how ignorant that sounds? Now, my friends who do smoke weed are a mixture of all ethnicities, yet they are not prejudged. I didn't realize hair would be so crucial to my outer appearance. I simply got tired of perming my hair and/or putting fake hair in my head to have my hair look European. My hair has become my freedom because it is all natural and it gives me a sense of freedom from how society says I should look. It reminds me that I am beautiful with exactly the long locks that God has given me. My hair has even stopped me from being hired at some lucrative companies; my headhunter told me, "I could get you a job paying six figures, but you must change your hair. Can't you wear a wig or something?" Not all money is good money, especially if you're going to lose yourself in the process! Needless to say, I switched headhunters.

Believe it or not, men say they want a woman with their real hair, but I'm not sure they mean natural hair. I've been dating this Black gentleman for six months, who told me he really liked me, but he wanted to see my real hair. After six months of dating someone who has the same hairstyle, you would assume they'd know that's your real hair. Either way, he was unaware that this was my real hair.

I asked him, "What did you think was in my hair?"

"I just thought you had braids, yarn, or some sort of added hair." I laughed and he said, "Honey, I usually don't date people with hair like yours." And he's Black!

These are not braids or any type of additives. These are Sisterlocs, they are 100 percent natural and it is all my real hair. I thought, *My hairstyle won't change unless I cut the locs out. Now that you know my hairstyle won't change, will that change your feelings for me?* Yes, I know my hair is an acquired taste, but it is one of the features I love about myself! People like what they like! I'm not trying to conform for anyone any longer, not for my speaking engagements, my businesses, or my mate's opinions! Nothing is worth losing a part of yourself, especially one of the parts you love. Could you imagine changing yourself for someone or something that might only be seasonal? The only thing in life that is guaranteed is the love you have for yourself. Self-love is timeless and price-less.

My mate was used to dating women of other ethnicities or who wore weave. No matter how many perms wore or weaves I inserted in my head, I would never, could never, and will never be a "Becky with the good hair," as Beyoncé describes. If you want Becky, go for Becky. I love all ethnicities and I have dated a variety of races. So, I do not care who a person dates, the lesson I've learned is to thine own self be true! Still show respect to all ethnicities. Just because you like Becky doesn't mean you have to discredit and slander Bianca. Although racism exists, it is more painful when it exists within your own race. Ebony queens have been discredited so many times by neg-gas from the same race calling them dogs, bit**es, hoes, sluts, gold-diggers, and other derogatory names that have been used to brainwash society from loving the Ebony woman and destroying the true essence of Black love. If you ask another ethnicity how they view Black women, the answer is disheartening. But the caveat is no other race belittles their women on media—socially, musically, etc.—anywhere in the world the way Black men do while simultaneously stating that Black lives matter.

A lot of Black women will never experience marriage because the Ebony woman has truly been disgraced from her own race. Why would another race want what is not desired by their own? I suggest you read the book *The New Black Man Is the Black Woman* by Lana L. Forte, M.Ed. It reveals just how much responsibility a Black woman must carry, whether she wants to or not, due to the Black man not stepping up to the plate for her and his/their children. Other races will show their assets on sex tapes and interact with multiple men, and yet, consequently because they are of a different ethnicity, they are considered an asset and become the wives of multimillionaires and billionaires. Money, power, and success equate to being able to afford a different persuasion on your arm.

Wonder if you love a Black woman, how would you be perceived? I have white friends, Hispanic friends, and other ethnicities who will only date Black men. Black men and men of other races will only date certain type of women, so again, this is not a bashing chapter. It is to open the eyes of those who will not even speak to women of their own race and who look down on the Ebony mothers who birthed them because they have been brainwashed to hate all Ebony women. Look at commercials, movies, sitcoms, billboards, social media . . . Very few families are truly displayed as a dark-complected African American couple. Love who you love, but respect everyone; a "good morning" does not cost a dime. When I lived in California, Ebony men would look left just to ignore a Black woman walking on the right, and they would barely speak while avoiding eye contact. In Atlanta the Ebony men speak freely, and they make you feel like a human being. Do you realize if all African American men stopped dating African American women, the African American race would eventually die? It is already in the making. Look around and see the increase of biracial relationships promoted on TV. Again, I love people that love me, so this is just pointing out some of the changes that have been occurring.

Do you have a diverse group of friends? Do you have different categories of friends? Rich, poor, religious, party animal, homebody—if so, this is a healthy inclusion model you're establishing in your personal world. Each race has their law-abiding citizens, those who dress professionally, those who take pride in their overall appearance, people of valor, integrity, ethics, and morals. Then you have those who are misfits—their appearance is uncouth, they do not take pride in their overall way of life, they're thieves, liars, or manipulators with a get-over mentality; it's not unique to one set of people.

Imagine getting on an elevator with a person who appears dangerous, smells badly, is drooling out of his mouth, his pants are sagging, his eyes and teeth are yellowish. This person is getting on the elevator with you at nighttime. Notice I never described his race—would it matter? No, you would be apprehensive and frightened of the potential negative outcome. Color has no barrier; you would be fearful just the same. So, let's change our perspective of people and look at one's actions instead of only their outer appearance. Of course, you need to be cautious, but don't be so quick to judge. We all must share this world. Why not be united instead of divided?

Now, sometimes we confuse racism, prejudice, discrimination, and division with simply not being the right fit for certain opportunities. For example, have you ever observed a casting call for a movie when they have a role in mind? They have a set description for the character trying out for specific parts. Could you imagine Tyler Perry playing the role of Donald Trump? Could you imagine Joe Biden playing Dr. Martin Luther King Jr.? Some roles are not discriminatory, they simply call for a distinctive person suited for a specific role. The same is true in real life. The essence of an individual should be determined before you decide where and if they can fit in your world.

As I was writing this chapter, my daughter had a homework assignment similar to this title, called "Is America Racist?" I thought it would be apropos to see a fifteen-year-old's perspective. See the bonus chapter featuring Genesis RoyalGE Jean.

Love yourself, especially the color of your skin, because it is not going to change!

In conclusion, it took a long time to understand that racists are the problem, not me, which adds to the R.A.W. transformational viewpoint. See, we each were created to be an original. When I look in the mirror, I own that I am an African American female with Sisterlocs. That is the first thing I see and that you observe before I open my mouth. Yes, I am educated, beautiful inside and out, curvaceous, financially fit, and I have a zeal for life. These are the attributes you will only get to know after I open my mouth and heart to share them with you. I OWN who I am, and I will not change to meet another human's standards nor apologize for my stance. Once I owned my truth and stopped trying to be something I am not, I began to view racism as just that! The truth is it exists it is not going anywhere, but you have the choice to participate or not. Yes, it is that easy, love or hate, black or white, it is a choice. Many racists were born to be that way; it is a learned behavior. It may sound cheesy, but I choose love. I prefer to be in the company of people who gravitate toward me and me them. Don't take it personally; not everyone will like you no matter how hard you try, regardless of race, culture, or status. I was a people-pleaser for years, but you cannot please everyone, and not everyone will like you, nor will you care for everyone. It is true that racism exists, but you don't have to bow down to supremacist theories.

Racism is both individualized and systemic, and it is intertwined in every institution in America. So, focus on not judging a book by its cover but by the content, the script, and most importantly the character and integrity within. The abuse of racism is not going anywhere, so search your heart and find out how you can best survive and thrive in a world that does judge you by many of the images we cannot change. Make sure you are doing your part! Analyze your circle, join diverse groups to get to know people who don't have your skin color but do possess your heart. The world is a melting pot. We are often brainwashed how to view people, especially through the power of persuasion, the news, social media outlets, and old ideology. All I suggest is to be openminded! The only person you can change is you. Focus on loving yourself and embracing all of who you authentically are and walk past those who don't embrace you as if they were invisible. Hate is hard to ignore, but it gets easier with time. Also, make a conscious decision to become a part of something bigger than you to assist with the incremental changes necessary to develop into large changes. Don't just talk about it, be about it. Paint your legacy for the next generation no matter how minute. One drop of water multiplied creates an ocean. Create your ripple!

Keep in mind, if you have people who are completely and utterly disrespecting you, you cannot close your eyes and ignore their piercing, malicious words or deeds. Reach out to organizations and ask for specific help to guide you to fight without using your fists, but instead using your words and defending your inalienable rights through the judicial system to reveal and change these atrocities. Believe it or not, some lawyers fight for everyone to have equal opportunity, and these like-minded people always keep on board.

CHAPTER 6 SELF-EVALUATION AND NOTES

1) Do you agree or disagree that racism, discrimination, or division exists? Explain.

_____

_____

_____

_____

_____

_____

_____

2.) Do you feel like racism or unjustifiable treatment exists toward you? Why?

_____

_____

_____

_____

_____

_____

_____

3) Have you spoken to anyone about your feelings? If so, what happened?

4) Do you have racism in your heart for others? If so, explain.

5) Analyze your truth, own it and write down all the personal mistreatments you've encountered over the years (use more pages if needed). After this exercise, if your anger is unresolved, call the hotline listed at the end of this chapter for further professional assistance catered to your needs.

Notes

Purge:	Get rid of unwanted feelings
Emerge:	Rise from the situation
Surge:	Propel your pain into power and purpose

Assignment: Write how you will
PURGE, EMERGE, then SURGE.

_____

_____

_____

_____

_____

_____

_____

_____

_____

_____

_____

_____

_____

NATASHAY STARR

EEOC Equal Employment Opportunity
Commission: (877) 497-5866

CHAPTER 7
HURT PEOPLE HURT PEOPLE

Have you dated someone who was scarred from being abused, adopted, molested, traumatized, confused with their sexuality, promiscuous, a user, a loser, an abuser, or simply a toxic person?

Yes, I have dated all the above! I was that girl who thought love would be easy. You meet someone, fall in love, and the Disney love story would unravel. I thought I was going to meet my husband in college, get married, have four kids, a Shih Tzu dog, and a white picket fence, and live happily ever after. WAKE UP! Although that does happen, what is the likelihood of it happening that perfectly? Please turn off the fairy tales in your head. Many of us have been brainwashed about how falling in love should happen. What is the truth? Any love worth building will take longer than the fantastical and blissful love connection in a two-hour Disney movie. It takes agape love, time, compromise, communication, and patience.

Over the years, I've dated all the men I described, and I wondered why every time I opened my heart and fell for someone quickly, I ended up hurt. Was it where I was meeting them? Did I attract hurt people because I was hurt? Was it the way I looked, the way I dressed? Was it my pheromones, my aura, or in my DNA? Was I cursed? I once read that single people wear the letter "D" (desperate) on their forehead when they are ready for marriage, and they are in search of their ultimate soulmate. Yes, I want marriage, but I discovered I was wearing the ultimate "D" on my forehead. Did I really want love, marriage, and family so badly that I was accepting anyone who paid me the slightest bit of attention? So, I'd wear my blindfolds and ignore their toxicity and fool myself into believing, at least at the onset, that they cared and that I could love their hurt away and make them whole. Ultimately, I just wanted to say I DO!

Have you noticed the person you don't want wants you, but the one you want doesn't? The one loving person who is attractive, intelligent, sexy, a provider, and who always makes you happy—they're typically the one you want, yet they don't view you in the same light. Yes, there is something wrong with this picture! Hmmm, why do you think that is? Since the person you want doesn't want you, do you hurt the person who wants you, not purposefully but subliminally?

I kept asking myself, what is wrong with me? I have dated some extraordinary men as well as other unique individuals, but something kept happening in my relationships leaving me more alone and more broken each time. I began to evaluate myself. Yes, I say when the same thing keeps happening to you and you are the only common denominator, you must review and evaluate your steps to ensure you are in a head space to give love and receive love. The best place to start is with a relationship counselor or therapist to learn the theory behind your behavior. While simultaneously getting off the merry-go-round of dating until you get a clear understanding and can remedy some intrinsic beliefs and behaviors.

My first step was seeking a counselor. My counselor was thorough; she took me to my childhood to learn about my upbringing and the male role models in my life. Imagine being in your mother's womb and your mother is at the abortion clinic about to end your life. My dad comes to save the day and tells my mom his family will raise the child so they can finish college. My grandmother and poppy on my mother's side said they would raise me also. The spirit of rejection was immediately instilled in me as a child. It's something I didn't ask for, but this challenge has followed me to this very day. I was wanted by my grandparents, but there is nothing like a biological mother's love and dad's love. My mom was twenty years old, in college, and she had decisions to make that would impact both of our lives. Gratefully, my mother felt me kick in her and toss and turn in her belly, and that's when my mother began to bond with me and she knew she couldn't let me go! She kept me and moved from Iowa to Atlanta to raise me the way she saw fit, without any interference from my dad and grandparents.

As a child, again, I felt rejected because my dad was not in the same state, though he would always send money and gifts on off-seasons because he was a Jehovah's Witness. (It was another form of rejection having no birthday, Christmas, or other holiday gifts from him, which I didn't understand as a child, and it did hurt.) My mother was either dating men of elevated financial status or married to them: Universal's vice president, a Hawks player, original Drifters, a pharmaceutical salesman, and my daddy, the chief of police. Each male expressed their love to me by trying to impress my mother and buy both of us extravagant gifts. They would always give me money, not small change but stacks of money to go shopping, get my hair done, and do as I please. Don't laugh, but I really thought money grew on trees because it seemed endless, and I began to equate money and gifts with love.

For this reason, I believed all men had money. I grew up expecting men who cared for me to spoil me and give me money and gifts to demonstrate their love and affection; the bigger the gift, the more they loved me. This was the tag line forming in my psyche. As I was describing several of these incidents to my counselor, she began to dissect my past. She advised me to read The Five Love Languages by Gary Chapman. This book helped me to understand more about myself and the love languages I subscribe to! I strongly suggest you read this book to find out your love language. Mine is affirmation, acts of service, and gifts. The counselor also noted that all the men in my life showered me with love through gift-giving, therefore, she said, "You have been conditioned to equate love with gifts." If a man never does anything for me but earf**k me, he will not be able to last long in my life, not because I am a gold-digger but because I believe a man will invest in what they believe in: stocks/bonds, gadgets, houses, cars. This same theory should be applied to investing in his love interest.

Now, when you are in an unhealthy relationship, you only see it from the inside. So, I am telling you a story from the outside looking in. True story, once upon a time, my mother started to date again after an eight-year hiatus. Yes, my mother is absolutely beautiful, but heartbreaks tore her down internally. It may not have been reflected in her looks, but it was reflected in her guarded existence. This handsome, charming man came from Heaven, literally, and he was smitten with my mother. He was everything my mother prayed for and manifested in her journal. Their first date was like watching two teenagers dating without any of the baggage that came from life experiences. We had a picnic at the lake, and we double-dated. Her guy brought her flowers, her favorite fruit, favorite food, and drink of choice. We played cards, had fun chatter, and got to know each other in an exhilarating atmosphere. They quickly became inseparable because he worked from home and so did she. Therefore, he could work from her house, which especially brought them together during COVID-19, while the state was locked down.

He started working from her house quite a bit. Then he started to buy products to repair items in my mother's home. Granted, she'd had her home for over eighteen years, and yes, it needed some assistance, but I was not expecting him to ask for a honey-do list, every day, but he did, just so he could fix or buy all the projects or secret desires of my mom's heart. If she thought it, he would immediately supply it. At this point I was leery. Was he bugging the house? Some IT reps know how to bug your house and watch your every move and listen to your conversations. This relationship was moving way too fast! However, watching them glow, grow, and travel in sync restored much in my soul toward believing in the possibility of true love.

From nowhere, the red flags began swarming like bees. This man, an IT specialist, immediately made me skeptical of his actions. I became like one of the investigators on *Forensic Files*. I had never seen a man move so fast! He took her on all-expense-paid trips, provided multiple shopping sprees, bought new furniture, and fixed things around the house. Gradually one closet turned into two closets full of his clothes, yet they weren't living together. Keep in mind, he was still treating my mother golden, as well as all of us butterfly girlz (Grandma had a butterfly wing, my mother a wing, myself, and my daughter had a wing). What was his game plan? Could he truly be falling for my mother at this accelerated pace? From the outside looking in, my mother had finally met an extraordinary man. Well, I still was concerned no matter how charming he was. I told my mother to keep some of her feelings in reserve but go for it with her eyes wide open. I did tell him if he ever was no longer interested in my mother, to leave without physically harming her. I could help her mend, but physical hurt warrants a different reaction. He agreed!

This man had been raised in an ultra-abusive foster home because his biological mom chose a new husband over her children, and she put all of her children out to pasture. Remember—hurt people hurt people.

I believe the whirlwind of love started in May around Mother's Day and ended in September. This situation almost destroyed my mother. She was shaking uncontrollably, one of her eyes was swollen—not from being beat, but neurologically swollen. He had picked up two closets full of clothes, amongst other items, and he told my guy friend and me it just didn't work out. He left without any feelings of remorse. Where was all the charm and loving personality? What happened to communication? What was the point of leaving so abruptly, so cold and heartless?

Yes, he quickly exited my mother's life and never gave her proper closure. He informed us that he was moving out of the country, which he often did because he could work from anywhere in the world. We later found out this was part of his pattern of brokenness. If I had to guess, I would say he met another woman. Either way, he hurt my mother, and he will end up hurting the new victim as well. Yes, hurt people hurt people. And, unfortunately, these people have been so damaged that they're afraid to love and truly don't know how to love themselves nor others because they've never experienced love but only cruelty all their lives. The stats on these types of adults have grown exponentially due to the instability of the nuclear family and alternate living styles.

Have you noticed any similar situations in your life? How can you date someone for five months, but the breakup pain can last for five years? Releasing the anger someone caused you is not easy! Writing this book has been therapeutic for me, therefore I suggest you journal your hurt or write your own book to tell your story. You are not the only one who has experienced this degree of broken promises and hurt. You are not alone! There comes a time when we must take responsibility for our own actions. Yes, many people find love online and move fast. Yes, it can happen to you, but be blatantly honest with yourself and be cognizant of when a person displays signs of a history of coming from a broken home, or being broken-hearted and hurt in life, repeatedly without healing, yes, hurt people hurt people; danger! Consider doing a background check with a credible company to solidify if your potential partner is single, identify their criminal history, and examine any other topics of interest. I strongly suggest doing this investigative work earlier on in the relationship. Gather the facts.

Be honest with yourself! Are you still hurt from your past relationships? Do you feel bitter from life's curve balls? Are you broken and do you have emotional issues? Timing is everything. Maybe now isn't the right time to date but to work on yourself. Find a counselor, someone who specializes in relationships, and remember that not all therapists are the same. Learn to laugh at some of your experiences, good, bad, or indifferent. I used to be embarrassed about some of my past. Now, I laugh and channel those feelings into my upcoming dating book, which will share some of the unique dating experiences that took me on my journey of being hurt, to hurting others, to healing and focusing on turning past hurts into life lessons. Use this new day to elevate yourself and elevate others, and love will come to you! Stop hurting people and allowing people to hurt you!

CHAPTER 7 SELF-EVALUATION AND NOTES

1). Are you the one who hurts people, gets hurt, or both? Explain.

_____

_____

_____

_____

_____

_____

_____

2) Why do you think the hurt occurred? Does it keep happening in the same way? Explain.

_____

_____

_____

_____

_____

_____

_____

_____

3) Do you and your partner(s) have a history of past hurt? If yes, explain.

_____

_____

_____

_____

_____

_____

_____

_____

4) Do you have any relationship role models? If so, do you mimic their relationships?

_____

_____

_____

_____

_____

_____

_____

_____

5) Make a pros and cons list of what you like and dislike about you and your partner. Be honest so you can release the anger and move into a healthy relationship.

_____

_____

_____

_____

_____

_____

_____

Notes

_____

_____

_____

_____

_____

_____

Purge:	Get rid of unwanted feelings
Emerge:	Rise from the situation
Surge:	Propel your pain into power and purpose

Assignment: Write how you will
PURGE, EMERGE, then SURGE.

Join our R.A.W. Transformation family for support.

CHAPTER 8
DEALING WITH LOSS, BEREAVEMENT

Do you know about hospice? Do you know what bereavement is? I thought I knew, until I was hired as a hospice sales consultant. My definition of hospice was simple; it was a scary word that only meant death! Hospice care is so much more. It is a service that provides quality end-of-life care. If you have a loved one who is experiencing incurable ailments, locate a reputable hospice company, check ratings and reviews, then call to see if your loved one qualifies for this service. Hospice companies provide extraordinary services such as a registered nurse and hospice aide visits up to three to five times a week, free medicine, social worker assistance, free medical equipment, spiritual advisors and guidance, bereavement counselors, respite care, and volunteers. Hospice organizations focus on the care of the patient, but they listen to the needs of family members, as well. The team will also answer any questions you may have, offer suggestions for funeral preparations, and help to ensure the customer's will is in order—and all these extraordinary services are all covered 100 percent by Medicare. (This is subject to change based on your insurance.) So, speak to your primary care doctor or call a hospice consultant. The service is amazing!

While I was working in hospice care, I noticed that people losing a loved one had a bereavement counselor with them before, during the transition, and after their loss. The families told me the counseling was helpful to them. I encourage everyone experiencing the gradual transition of a loved one to speak to a bereavement counselor because the hurt, pain, and sadness can slowly cause depression and other health issues if not properly treated. I believe I was meant to work in hospice to share with the families how important hospice and bereavement counseling are and to expand my knowledge in this area.

I wish I had known about hospice when my grandparents were declining. Do you ever stop mourning the death of your parents? Siblings? Other family and friends? When my grandparents passed away, although it was sad for me and even sadder for my mother, I feel like they lived a full life. My grandmother died in her nineties. I loved them both very much, especially my grandmother. She sacrificed her life to serve God, her husband, children, and grandchildren, but never received the love she gave. She was very selfless. My mother is still torn from the death of her parents, and I encouraged her to seek out a bereavement counselor (someone who specialized in bereavement). This service is provided to family members free of charge with hospice care. When my mother went to a few bereavement sessions, she claimed it contributed to 90 percent of her healing along with God and prayer. So, no, we never get over missing our loved ones, but we can move on to continue writing our chapters in our lives with them as a guiding force.

Have you lost a loved one or several loved ones? I never took the time to understand the hurt I was feeling with the different deaths I experienced in addition to my grandparents. I started to reflect on some deaths I had never properly mourned. I reminisced on who passed away and how it had affected me. I lost my stepfather from lymphoma—he was my earth angel who taught my mom how to discipline me, and he loved me beyond reproach. Then my auntie, who was very special to us, died without warning from kidney failure in her late thirties. That was an unexpected shock right at Christmas. My soul mate died onsite after a car accident with an eighteen-wheeler. Recently, I lost loved ones unexpectantly. My stepsister was young and died from internal bleeding, and the last death that changed my life was my male cousin; he died from an enlarged heart at thirty-six years old, again unexpected. Here today and gone tomorrow.

The death of this male cousin, Majestic Royce Hamilton, was undeniably heartbreaking. We had a very close bond and worked on a lot of music and film projects together. Thankfully, he was able to live a full life and follow a lot of his dreams to fruition. His death changed me from playing it safe to following my dreams. When I die, I want to leave a legacy. I have bereaved my loss and I am chasing my dreams to live a full, purposeful life. Death often comes often unexpectedly. No one on earth knows how much time they have left, nor the hour of their death, so make each day count!

One of the tasks that has helped myself and others is to journal my daily emotions. Write down these feelings and give this exercise about ten minutes of your time every day. It gives you specific topics to discuss with your therapist and it also chronologizes your growth and changes with time. It's an easy exercise that has profound outcomes.

By working in the hospice field, the paramount lesson I learned is exactly how I view death. I had to have a paradigm shift in my thinking, from seeing death as the end to understanding and relishing in the fact that death is a part of life. It is the period to that person's chapter. I've retrained my brain to focus on the glorious memories, laughter shared, experiences treasured, and the accomplishments (young or old) of that person. I also practice giving "roses" to my loved ones, every chance I can get, while they are living so I will not have any remorse when they are gone. The guilt and extended sadness come in when you think of all the things you should have done but were too "busy" to do. Therefore, I alleviate that painful journey by doing right by people on a daily basis.

Also, because death is imminent to us all, make sure to assist those closest to you in arranging all their documents and insurance, being aware of their personal wishes around their hospitalization and burial, and know exactly where all pertinent information is located including banks and annuities. This way you can continue to honor that person when they're helpless and fulfill their vision of dying gracefully and with dignity. As we are witnessing, it's never too early to ascertain this knowledge, because death comes like a thief in the night and robs the young as well as the old.

Lastly, I've learned to check on those of the deceased on a regular basis and join them in celebrating the lives of their loved ones. With my grandmother, we went to her gravesite, where we prayed, exchanged funny memories of her, and released balloons as one way to acknowledge her memory and the profound impact she had on our lives. It not only was a beautiful ceremony, but it also helped me to release some of my longing for her to be still here in the flesh. Therefore, it was therapeutic to us all and a magnificent way to honor her.

Simply put, the present is a present. Live each day as such! Embrace every moment with yourself and with others as though it's your last, and you can't go wrong. For there are no guarantees that it just may be the last time you see that person, so make each of those moments count. Say and do exactly what your heart directs which will minimize having any regrets.

CHAPTER 8 SELF-EVALUATION AND NOTES

1) List the name, relationship, and time frame of the person who passed away.

_____

_____

_____

_____

_____

_____

2) Have you made time to deal with your loss? If so, how did you deal with each death?

_____

_____

_____

_____

_____

_____

_____

3) Are you harboring anger, depression, hate, or resentment? If so, how are you dealing with your feelings?

_____

_____

_____

_____

_____

_____

_____

_____

4) Do you have a peaceful understanding and acceptance of the death of your loved one(s)?

_____

_____

_____

_____

_____

_____

_____

5) To live and die is a part of life. Hypothetically, if given weeks to live, create a wish list:

_____

_____

_____

_____

_____

_____

_____

_____

Notes

_____

_____

_____

_____

_____

_____

_____

_____

Purge:	Get rid of unwanted feelings
Emerge:	Rise from the situation
Surge:	Propel your pain into power and purpose

Assignment: Write how you will
PURGE, EMERGE, then SURGE.

NATASHAY STARR

Join our R.A.W. Transformation family for support.

RELEASE ALL WITHIN:
YOUTH PERSPECTIVE
GENESIS "ROYALGE" JEAN
MOTIVATIONAL YOUTH SPEAKER

WHO IS GENESIS "ROYALGE" JEAN?

As of 2024, she is an eighteen-year-old, national honor roll student, who was born with a gift of helping youth who carry painful secrets, release all within. As she goes to college, I want her to use this book as a stepping-stone to walk the path of her purpose. Her natural ability to give sound advice comes from a power greater than me. Youth are wiser and I wanted to GIFT my daughter the opportunity to be part of my first book and use her story to help stop a child from ending their journey to soon!

IS AMERICA STILL RACIST?

Do you ever feel like you're being judged or made to feel unwelcome by your appearance when you go places? Well, I do. Being a brown-toned African American female can really break down your self-confidence because I feel judged by the color of my skin when entering certain areas. This issue is discussed throughout our country today. Which brings me to the question: is America still racist? It's a touchy subject that must be talked about because situations like George Floyd, Kendrick Johnson, the Black Lives Matter movement, Representative Park

Cannon, and others shouldn't be occurring today. That's why I would like to enlighten you about this issue. Some people believe racism is over, but I believe it's only getting worse.

Our country has faced and has overcome many challenges now and in the past. However, I feel as though the efforts to end racism and make EVERY citizen feel equal have failed tremendously. One of the reasons the Constitution was implemented was to make the citizens of our country feel safe and give citizens their rights, no matter what skin color they are. These were termed as inalienable rights, which are God-given rights that can never be taken away: the rights of life, liberty, and the pursuit of happiness. Which, by my calculation, have never been honored. Therefore, it baffles me when I hear people state, "Another Black male has been shot by the police" or "I'm afraid of the police because I'm Black." This is disheartening to hear from my peers and the people of our country, especially because I know the feeling of being discriminated against. This topic doesn't only apply to Black people but Middle Eastern people, Latinos, Asians, and many others.

This racism has a humongous impact on our nation today. According to an *Independent* article, "Rep. Park Cannon was arrested on Thursday after she knocked on Republican Gov. Brian Kemp's statehouse office door to protest the signing of the voting reform bill, which critics say is designed to make it harder for African Americans to vote." This statement has spoken for itself; this is one of the prime examples of racism today. Nowadays, people with power (predominantly Caucasian people) are covert racists, such as the Ku Klux Klan and other corporate, religious, political, and judicial institutions throughout America. For instance, they slide in little details in important documents that affect all Black American lives and paint a distorted picture where the whole Black culture is ostracized by the act of one. Our country is more racist today than back during the Emancipation Proclamation. The only difference is that people were more open with and accepting of this racist behavior, while today the person you sit next to can be the same person smiling in your face while simultaneously plotting against you because of their racist beliefs and standards.

George Floyd was a forty-six-year-old African

American man whose death was recorded. This African American was held down with force by a Caucasian officer according to the YouTube video "I Can't Breathe." The crime he committed was not as great as the crime of being born of a darker persuasion. The temporary crime would have landed Mr. Floyd some time in jail yet, he would have still been alive. The negligence of the officer ended up costing Mr. Floyd his life. It is evident the officer held Mr. Floyd down with his foot until he could no longer breathe, but the defense attorney attempted to discredit Mr. Floyd. According to an article in the Post-Gazette, "Mr. Floyd died of a heart condition and illegal drug use." The media has been known to sabotage the credibility of African Americans by portraying us as ignorant thugs. The news focuses on the one person of color who looks a mess, has no teeth, speaks Ebonics, and dresses like a homeless person, while overlooking an intelligent, well-groomed Black person.

Racism—as President Biden so succinctly put in his address on Tuesday, April 20, 2021—is alive and well. The verdict with the officer versus George Floyd is merely the first, minute step toward justice. The president explicitly explained that this is the first step toward justice, but we must remember this death as a barometer to change our thinking and our ways for eternity. Mindsets, laws, and behaviors must be changed on a holistic level in order to recognize and acknowledge that all men are created equal according to our Constitution. But will we as the *United* States of America ever really ever be united when in many ways we are divided? Should we rename our country the Un-United States of America?

HURT PEOPLE HURT PEOPLE

Although I am a young teenager, I have felt the hurt from not feeling the love of my father. My dad did his best, but sometimes your best isn't good enough. He always lived in another state. Therefore, he would send me money and gifts, but we didn't have the bond I longed for. I must admit his accent was undeniably hard to understand. He is from Haiti, and he speaks fluent Creole and broken English. He always called me his princess, but something was just missing from our relationship. I love my dad, but you know that feeling of hurt that lies in you, the small pain that never goes away. The one you feel when you have one parent showers you with love and the other is almost nonexistent. My Mom often said that I would have been a "Daddy's Girl" because I so longed for the love of my dad.

Well, I started to date, and most people try to find someone like their father. I didn't know what to look for and my mother taught me a lot of things, especially what to run away from, but no one could tell me who to be attracted to. The first person I was attracted to was so sweet and very much a giver. He spoiled me with gifts, and he started to share with me a story that his ex-girlfriend committed suicide. The more I learned about him, the more I could tell he was broken. I became his unpaid therapist. I guess the gifts were compensation, but he was truly broken, and we did not work out. I tried to remain his friend, but people are so hung up on the title of friend. Either way, we didn't work out.

The next person was very handsome. We worked together and he began to pursue me. It was so cute— he would call me and we'd talk on the phone for hours. We became inseparable. The longer we dated, the more I realized how troubled he was. His mom was strung out on drugs, and he had other family issues that went way beyond my counseling skills. It was rumored in his family that his grandpa just might be his dad. He was being raised by an aunt and the complications never seemed to stop. No matter the words of encouragement I gave him, he had seen and experienced too much in his seventeen years of life. He was just broken.

I noticed I attract hurt or broken people. Was I hurt and broken too? If so, how could I recognize it and turn it around? Be the person you would like to attract! So, if I am hurt and I attract hurt people, how do I change that around? And how can I help them without getting hurt myself? So many questions, and I would watch my mom pour into people and I realized I was doing the same thing. I started to notice I would uplift each broken person I met, and not just those two relationships, but males and females would come to me to get a dose of RoyalGE Roots or Genesis Guice (juice). If you come to me sad and hurt, I naturally see things differently and possess a natural gift of uplifting others but who was uplifting me?

I understand what my mother keeps telling me

about seasons. People come into your life for seasons, reasons, or forever. If you are hurt, try to fix it while it is in the beginning stages. Go to your school counselor if it is something light, listen to positive people, share your pain with your family or friends or someone you trust so both of you can deal with it. Listen to and study spiritual sermons and the Word. Hurt young people turn into horrific older people. Can you imagine holding on to hurt for fifteen, twenty, thirty years? Some hurt requires a therapist who specializes in your line of pain.

SUICIDAL SOCIETY: YOUTH

I received a phone call providing me the date of when my friend was going to kill himself. He added that if I told anyone, he would blame me and do it sooner. Well, what would you do? I prayed and I spoke to my mom about it, and she called a therapist. Suicide is different from offering a few words of encouragement; you have a limited time to stop that person from going through with it. The date was quickly approaching. The therapist made a few suggestions, but again, I was not supposed to tell anyone. Note to my friends and fans, I can keep a secret, but let's get real—could you imagine your friend saying they are going to kill themselves because they have nothing to live for? Yes, let's deal with that. I'll get into my stories, but think about your life. What do you have to live for? Knowing this becomes critical when you undergo major challenges. Some people don't have suicidal thoughts, so I am only referring to the people who think they have nothing to live for.

Suicidal thoughts cross all barriers of class, race, and religions; I know this because I went to some top-notch schools. Sadly, mean-hearted people are everywhere, and the pain people cause holds no limitations. I experienced several memorable episodes that knocked the wind out of me. But I will only share a few that might help you identify with how an innocent beginning can change a person's feelings toward life.

My first friend ever was the first of many to show me how people can change and cause hurt beyond repair. I hadn't seen my best friend in a while, and when I finally got to see her, she had so many friends she forgot me. It was only about a month since we had been apart and all I talked about at home was

Norma. When I got to her birthday party, I ran to her to embrace her, but she didn't even remember my name. I was left all alone at her party because I didn't know anyone else. I felt very isolated. Thankfully, my mother took me home instead of allowing me to stay at the slumber party. I was also the only African American at the party, so it was a double whammy. I did not want to commit suicide, but those small incidents pierce you and start a wall of boundaries and the feeling of defeat and rejection at such an early age.

Later, another friend and I were in the third grade. On Monday she was my friend, but by Thursday she told everyone to go to the playground the next day and bring their phones because she was going to beat up Genesis. Well, she was just my friend! My mom made me call her and ask her what happened and why she changed. Worst mistake ever! Let me describe this girl. She was four times my size and she didn't have any hair; she was hard-looking, and I was thin and small. I had never fought, and I was secretly scared to fight her, especially on camera. This girl had nothing to lose! She was doing bad in school, and I was on the A & B honor roll and presidents' list. Years later I learned the ugly truth about jealousy and how no matter how kind you are to people, they will simply like you or dislike you for no apparent reason or fault of your own but due to their own insecurities.

This process followed me through elementary, middle, and high school, and even to work. I would meet a homegirl, we would develop a bond, and something would go wrong. She would smile in my face and pick me for information, and then take my information and use it negatively, usually to gossip and spread my secrets. I developed tough skin and I actually was forced to become a loner, an introvert. I often would feel sad and simply wonder what was wrong with me. Why couldn't I keep friends who were loyal and had my back instead of causing trouble?

I had been bullied in my earlier years, been threatened for lunch money, and by now I considered myself tough. I had gone through trials and tribulations to make me strong. As an only child, I got into my own self-pity. *Woe is me . . . my dad was not physically around.* These mishaps cause a person to feel depressed and contribute to contemplating what the world would be like without them in it. Many of my friends who have school drama, family drama, or just feel like something is missing have often told me they understand why some kids follow through with suicide. And their stories are a lot more devastating than mine; they're things no child should see, let alone experience!

No, my story is not as bad as it could be. But my mom has taught me not to compare myself to anyone, because I am uniquely me. However, in this case, it has helped me to realize that my life hasn't been so bad. Some stories from your peers will make you cry: their mama didn't want them, both parents are on drugs, a grandpa might be my friend's dad. It goes on and on. My conclusion is to own your pain and what you feel so you can overcome whatever it is you're going through and get all the facts to put everything in perspective. I have had several incidents that happen way worse than my earlier years, but the trials I experienced when I was younger prepared me for now! I am strong, independent, and intelligent, and I have confidence that I have earned and learned. I look to build people up, not tear them down. I learned this from my mother. I learned that even though my dad lives all the way in California, and I don't see him much, he really does love me, and he shows me through constantly calling me, buying things I need or want, and always bragging about me to his family and friends. It took growing up to come to that conclusion. So, take all those lemons of life, the sour, hurtful episodes, and squeeze out all the juice and make lemonade out of it so it becomes that much sweeter (I know . . . I'm sounding like my mom).

Now, I hang with people who consistently show me love. My friends are mainly guys, and several of them are gay or bisexual. They have just proven to be loyal to me. Just learn to love yourself and watch the type of people you attract. You are who you hang around! If all of your friends are depressed, you will become depressed; if your friends are doing well in life, you will thrive or strive to do well. If you hang with friends who do drugs or have sex, well, you get the point!

* * *

Looking at my daughter, she had something far worse than I did—social media! I understand being treated unfairly by your peers is a painful process, especially when you're not a trouble starter. I'm not sure why some people are loved by all and the ones that everyone loves are typically mean but popular individuals. Stay in tune with your children and these situations so you can use this as a teachable moment, and you can lovingly lick the wounds away even while you're holding back your own tears of the hard life lessons that your child is experiencing and possibly similar ones that you, as the parent, may have even experienced.

Remember, many schools are understaffed. Do not leave it to the educators to determine if your child is contemplating suicide. If you do notice a change worth being concerned about, feel free to be proactive. Research youth and see how many kids are committing suicide a year. If you are thinking about suicide yourself, just call the hotline (988).

RESOURCES

Disclosure: We have no affiliation with any of the resources listed. This list is to be used at your discretion. Resource information is subject to change at any time. If the information changes, please let us know. It truly takes a team. For life-threatening emergencies, please call 911.

RAPE IS REAL

National Sexual Assault Hotline

1-800-656-HOPE (4673)

VICES VARY

Free Drug & Alcohol Addiction Hotline 24/7

855-315-4766

A national, free, twenty-four-hour hotline providing resources for Drugs and Alcohol.

SAMHSA's Substance Abuse and Mental Health National Helpline

1-800-662-HELP (4357) (also known as the Treatment Referral Routing Service), or TTY: 1-800-487-4889

A confidential, free, 24-hour-a-day, 365-day-a-year resource.

SUICIDAL SOCIETY

National Suicide Prevention Hotline:

800-273-8255 (TALK)

Stop!!! A temporary situation will never be resolved with a permanent death.

Suicide and Crisis Lifeline

Call or text the 988 Suicide and Crisis Lifeline

This is a free twenty-four-hour national hotline that provides support for those in distress and crisis.

CHURCH CRISES

Catholic Bishop Abuse Reporting Service

1-800-276-1562

https://reportbishopabuse.org/

WORK WARS

Equal Employment Opportunity Commission (EEOC)

(877) 497-5866

Discrimination against equality

RACISM EXISTS

Equal Employment Opportunity Commission (EEOC)

(877) 497-5866

Discrimination against equality.

HURT PEOPLE HURT PEOPLE

National Institute of Mental Health

1-866-615-6464, 8:30 a.m. – 5 p.m. ET, M-F nimhinfo@nih.gov

SAMHSA's Substance Abuse and Mental Health National Helpline

1-800-662-HELP (4357) (also known as the Treatment Referral Routing Service), or TTY: 1-800-487-4889 A confidential, free, 24-hour-a-day, 365-day-a-year resource.

DEALING WITH LOSS, BEREAVEMENT

Certified Transformational Coach & Bereavement Counselor, Natashay Starr & Team host sessions, retreats, and programs to guide willing people to overcome personal obstacles.

ACKNOWLEDGMENTS

A legacy is a memorandum you want to leave so your generation and generations thereafter will know who Natashay Starr really is and learn what I have overcome. Writing this book has been therapeutic, a release beyond compare, and it has repaired and renewed my soul. I first would like to thank my God, Jesus, my Holy Spirit, my Angels, and all Heavenly entities and the greatness of the supernatural forces that have worked on my behalf. Thank you for blessing me with the time and ongoing revenue to begin writing my book in Sacramento. Each day I felt stronger and restored enough to move away from self-pity and to transform my "truths" into helping myself and others identify with the anger, guilt, pain, hurt, and other dysfunctions holding me back from moving toward my purpose, success, and intrinsic fulfillment.

This is my first book, therefore my acknowledgments will be similar to a singer or rapper winning their first Grammy—long, yet meaningful to the individual. My daughter, Genesis, a.k.a. RoyalGE, made me want to become a better person from the time I found out I was pregnant. I stopped wearing fake hair and got Sisterlocs while she was in my belly. I wanted my daughter to see and know the REAL me, and I thought real hair would be the start.

Genesis, my one and only child, I love you so much and you are my gift from God. You are destined to do great things! Genesis, "RoyalGE," you're my ride-or-die daughter and I love you, my beautiful princess, more than words can express. I am a proud mother and blessed for you to be so talented—rapping, singing, dancing, acting, modeling, and hopefully preaching—you have that gift. My butterfly girl. I must thank her father, Beker, for giving me a great gift, GG, her nickname to me: God's Gift.

This next person is my Earth Angel, my cheerleader every single step of the way, my earthly rock, my ride-or-die, mother, sister, BMSF (Best Mom Sister Friend): my mother, Lana L. Forte, M. Ed. She has been my role model, is a retired educator and principal, authored three books, traveled the world, and worked two jobs off and on throughout her life to support me. She always encouraged me to rap, write, and love, and even prevented me from indulging in my suicidal thoughts. She's been there every step of the way to pour great words of wisdom and sincere love deep within me. Mom, I could not have survived this world without you as my mom and my butterfly girl. I love you with my whole heart!

Thank you, Dad, and my stepmom. Charles and JO have been loving, kind, amazing Jehovah's Witnesses. You have always put God first and followed his rules by living an exemplary life. Dad, I must say they truly broke the mold when they made you. You gave me the first Bible that I ever understood, and I still read it to this day. Jehovah's Witnesses are extraordinary examples of the pillar of righteousness. I love you, Dad and stepmom. I appreciate you both and am grateful to have you in my life.

RIP Grandma Rosa, "Sexy Chocolate" (I was able to read this to her before she passed away). You believed in me so much that you invested in me without hesitation. You were the first person who said I have a problem with the way I treat men. You told me to make amends with my father because that would help close the gap in my life with how I viewed men.

You always made me evaluate my motives and myself. I love every bit of your being, Grandma, especially when I beat you in Scrabble and cards! Thank you for our talks, hugs, and for just being so loving to my daughter and me. You had a chance to leave earth, but you said you knew the grandkids would need you, so you stayed on a while longer. I thank you for staying on this earth longer for me. I love you, butterfly girl. Please continue to watch over me from Heaven.

To the rest of my family: Each of you means so much to me in different ways. Poppy, rest in peace (he is my grandfather). He gave me nicknames that started my identity crises, lol. I love ya, Poppy. My Aunt Venus (RIP), Uncle Mark (RIP), Uncle David, my uncle who used to teach me how to fight. I beat up this boy so bad I left him with a bloody nose and black eye. Cousin Shaun and fam, Cousin Royce and fam, Cousin Preston, Austin, Dustin, Hamilton, Donavan, Starr, Dominique, my immediate first-generation cousins and family, my Great Auntie Helen, Great Uncle Sonny (RIP). My cousins Debbie, Lori, and Milton. My God family, JoJo, Avery, Iisha, Simmone, Kim M, Chelsea, Chad, and all my other cousins and family from Atlanta to Iowa and throughout the world, especially the Hamiltons, McDonalds, Sharps, Greens, etc. All my family members and friends, thank you for believing in me and supporting all of my dreams.

Our family has been dealt some roadblocks and I bind up any generational curses that have not truly allowed our family bloodline to excel and prosper with the enormous talents that we've been given. I pray these generational spiritual chains are broken in our entire bloodline and the bloodlines going forward. We will see all our gifts, talents, and treasures multiply now and in all generations to follow. We are talented, successful, God-loving servers, multimillionaires/billionaires, and beacons of light used to help others find their way. May our family and friends join as a new generation of thinkers. Not everyone can soar like an eagle, but I'm praying that our family will elevate with wings to fly! I am prepared to love all who love me and release all who do not have my best interests at heart.

To my female friends: Melinda W. B., you have been my friend since seventh grade. You've loved me in all stages of my life, and I have loved you as well. You know my secrets and I know yours. Our friendship has been tested, but I believe we have grown from our past mistakes. My sister, I love you and I am glad we have grown up to be beautiful women of integrity and that you are the godmother to my daughter. You were always my best sistah cheerleader. Thank you for your love and support.

Teresa "Cookie," thank you for dreaming with me and being my prayer warrior. You were the only person who really understood my dreams and aspirations because you wanted this success as much as I did. I never met anyone who wanted a successful life as bad as me until I met you. This is how Cookie and I roll: Ring, ring. "Hi, this is multimillionaire Cookie, how may I help you?" "Hi, this is Tyler P's business partner and I read your play and I want you to be on my team. Can you come meet me in an hour?" "Well, I'm in London at the moment finishing up a project with Opraaaah, filming a reality show about helping others, but I can be at your studio by next Monday." We would do this for hours and never get tired of dreaming. As a man thinketh, so he shall become. In addition, Cookie was my prayer partner. We would fast and pray for each other. We tried multiple entrepreneur ventures together, and the fruits of our labor we'll soon harvest. I will always have love for you!

Daphnia W., you are one the baddest queens I know! I must tell your business, she had me reevaluate the men I date! Her king bought her an office complex, properties, high-end cars, and just set her up for success. Daph has property in Atlanta, Jamaica, Miami, and Africa, and probably will have more after you read this book. I know you did not know we would stay friends as long as we have, but I am glad to have you in my life. I wish you love, peace, and more prosperity.

DaVetta J., you always give words of encouragement and wisdom, thank you. I hope all your dreams, goals, and desires manifest beyond your wildest dreams. She will be styling me at times because she is one of the best-dressed feminine-quality queens I know. I pray you meet a husband who will cherish your phenomenal attributes.

Misti C., Cali, I appreciate you investing in me, because I could not have gone through my Sacramento journey without you, your love, and your support. You are a powerful, strong go-getter and a beautiful queen. You opened your doors to me and have been an Earth Angel in my life. I am grateful and proud to call you my friend! I look forward to going to the ocean and rekindling our friendship and sisterhood. You're a phenomenal woman and I can't thank you enough for how much love you've poured into me. I look forward to repaying you with a surprise!

CharterLIFE Team, you welcomed me with open arms, and I truly thank you for being an amazing team to work with!

Coach Sheya, thank you for starting me on this journey of writing my book! You've been such an inspiration to me and others who needed help writing their book. Thank you for giving me the support I needed. I look forward to working with you again.

Thanks to all the females who have impacted my life and helped me along the way. Thank you for entering my life and somehow impacting me more than you'll ever know. Whether it was for a season, reasons, or a lifetime, blessings, my sisters!

To my sober sisters and misters: I am only putting initials to respect our anonymity!

TJ, Cali, I met you on day two of my journey of turning my wine into water, lol. Thank you for making this transition fun. I gained weight because you can cook your butt off! But thank you for really embracing our new, developing friendship and opening your truths to me and allowing me to be truthful, too, while I was in a foreign land.

VM, Cali, you are so loving and wise. Thanks for kicking my butt and keeping me in shape to not only say I am sober, but also figure out how to stay sober. We developed an unspoken bond and sisterhood that will hold us accountable to making sober choices. I know I can call on and count on you, and I am here for you, as well. Thank you for being a special, intricate part of my life.

JSP, I will always have love for you. Your soul is purely for the intention of helping people stay sober. You are a warrior, an angel sent to earth to help those who suffer from alcoholism and learn newfound behavior. I never knew I had a problem until you broke it down to me with one of your detailed analogies, the ruler theory: Take out a ruler and on a scale of 1 to 12, tell me what number you are as an alcoholic. I said I was a 0.05—that was my first step. See, admitting I was an alcoholic is the first step. With this obsession it only gets worse, and you never get off the ruler until you die. The obsession never leaves. I love, value, and respect your doctrines. Thank you, JSP!

There are too many names to mention, but to all my other sober sisters and misters who helped me during this journey, thank you!

To the kings on my team: God has blessed me with some kings on my team, and I am blessed to really have men who love me for me.

Bishop P. Ivey, you always have my back and have felt my spirit, and you would call me to pray with me and for me. From day one we have been spiritually connected. Throughout our friendship, thank you for always pouring godly advice into me, praying with me and for me, and helping me see things through God's eyes, spiritual eyes not my own. You always poured words of greatness into me and told me you could see more than you could reveal. Thank you for being my encouragement, prayer warrior, and most of all, my friend.

Charles B., thank you for encouraging me to write this book and investing in my dream. You are an inspiration in my life. You have so many dreams and desires, and I hope to invest in them and help make your dreams a reality. I have watched you grow, spiritually by leaps and bounds. Our long, in-depth conversations have both motivated me and made me dig deeper. You have been a blessing in my life!

Fisherman, Jason. Wow! We fell in a brotherly love so fast; your wife accepted me with open arms, and I thank her for encouraging our friendship to bud. We have a purposeful connection! You were part of my dream team in my first radio podcast, and I am sure we are going to work together on many more projects! Keep thriving—you are working on your doctorate, and I am so proud of you! I will gift you all I learn during this journey because you will be the next role model for the world to hear.

Troy M., you have a way with words! Never assume, because you will make an ass of yourself. I learned a valuable lesson and I never again assume. Wishing you blessings with all your future endeavors.

Rob M., I always dreamed of being an entrepreneur, and you showed me it could, would, and did happen, not just with words, but you helped me start my business and you hired my company with weekly compensation. We've been through some things, but through the midst of it all, I know you've got my back and I have yours. Keep helping brothers elevate themselves and continue to be the blessing God called you to be. Wishing you happiness which surpasses all understanding!

Tamar P., you helped me to grow up and realize I had a few concerning issues that would hinder me the rest of my life if I didn't look deeper into them. Thank you for encouraging me to achieve my degree. You also took my daughter to every daddy-daughter dance when she was younger. You've been a real role model in our lives and a special man. I wish you and your wife ultra love and success. You are Martin and Malcom X combined— make a difference!

Norman P., thank you for showing me the finer things in life. You believed in me and encouraged me to know that I have greatness within and to not stop until it manifests. Our friendship has changed over the years on multiple levels, and I hope you get everything you ever dreamed of, because you are the only man I know who sacrificed his entire life for his child. I've watched you give up a prosperous life and turn lemons into lemonade. I never understood your focus until I had my own child. Your parenting skills are impeccable, and I am following in your footsteps. Congrats, Gabby is doing big things! I met her in elementary school and now she's graduated from college. Go, Daddy!

Everardo M., from New York, New Jersey, and Arizona to Atlanta, we've been through a lot! We allowed a lottery ticket to change our destiny. Not all money is good money! Thanks for believing in me and making it rain with hundreds of thousands of dollars. You are a superb man and I wish you and your family the absolute best! We never got it right, but knowing you are thriving, educated, a good father, and you're happily pursuing your dreams, goals, and plans is the best gift I could ask for!

Gabe W., I appreciate you! We are genuinely like brother and sister—we've run that line on a few people. I want to thank you for seeing my value and including me in all the business opportunities, mostly music and visions, that you have on the table. Entrepreneurship, entertainment industry, music, we just have a lot in common. I know the legal hustler in you is going to make a way out of any way, and I want to be a part of your success. Thanks for our cigar talks and prayers and for showing me that passion still exists. You set the bar high. I know your greatness, and I will not settle for less than the greatness you taught me to wait for.

ThomaSutra—so, this is what I've been missing? I have to publicly thank you for all of the words of wisdom and advice you have poured into me. I never knew the art of lovemaking until I met you! You introduced me to a new side of myself that I didn't know existed. You have prepared me for LOVE and I will forever be grateful! I will tell our story in my next book.

To my stepdad, Darnell J. You have been in my life since I was nine years old. You always call me your daughter and you are my real stepdad. Thank you for buying me my first car, taking me shopping for school, and simply spoiling my mother and me. You set the bar high. You made money seem like it grew on trees! I have not forgotten how you treated us when you were on top. Be on the lookout for the roles to reverse. I look forward to spoiling you! You're a great king on my team and my family, and I will always love you.

All the kings on my team, if I did not mention your name and you feel as though you impacted my life, thank you for your love and support!

Professionals: Dr. Carspecken (RIP) and team, you told me to go back to college and you taught me about saving, stocks, and bonds. You and the team that worked for you changed the course of my life in a positive way. I have never found someone who cared about their employees as much as you did. You showed me the true meaning of family away from family. Thank you for teaching me how to become the best version of myself and for being a great steward in my life. You failed me, because when Tyler Perry moved to your community before he was well known, you were supposed to introduce me to him. So you owe me a Tyler Perry intro! Lol. I love you, Dr. C. If you or the team ever need me, my doors are open to you!

Southkak (soundcloud.com/workmanmusic), you always had my back. Even when I tried to give up rapping, you would call me and put me on a song. You believed in me when I stopped believing in myself. I love you like a brother, and I know we are supposed to be extraordinarily successful together. I hope one day to call you like you called me and offer you a deal of a lifetime. Thank you for blessing me!

Eric T., we have been friends for a long time off and on. Thank you for teaching me tricks of the trade as far as writing and just having fun in the music industry. Man, I watched you just focus on your music, family, and helping others. You always had a good heart and I wish you continued success.

Geno W., you and I met at your father's garage sale, and we started making music together from the first moment we met. Literally, I was in your studio within that week to work on a song for LA Sno. You are so talented; this music game has hurt you and took some of your joy, but they can never take your talent. You are one of the most influential, talented singer/songwriters I have ever met. I pray that payday is on the horizon.

Gene G. (RIP), Paul W., and team—you signed me to Universal/Sounds of Atlanta, and it changed my life. He provided me with fifteen minutes of feeling what fame felt like. I enjoyed every single moment. Rest in peace and thanks for the moment. I am still waiting on my six-figure check . . .

Miracle—my rap buddy! I was blown away by our synergy. Even to this day we have a special bond that works well on and off the camera. You welcomed me with open arms, and I am grateful for sharing my first fifteen minutes of fame with you! I look forward to working with you again for our next chapter, especially helping others in need—we both share that in common. You have such a big heart.

Caliph S., you taught me to take my lyrical skills outside of just writing songs, but also out of my comfort zone to write books. You put me on several projects that launched my mindset and put me on a path that offers unlimited possibilities. I am forever grateful.

RIP Majestic Royce. I have saved the best for last! My extraordinarily talented cousin, I saw you teach yourself how to write songs, make music beats/tracks, photography, shoot videos, movies, everything you need in the entertainment industry. I have never been prouder to see my bloodline run through your veins. Thank you for my "cousin discounts," but I always paid you so you would know I believe in your work, and I KNOW you are my Angel looking over me! Cuz, I will keep our legacy of helping the family tree change financially and spiritually. I miss you and I will always love you and your family!

Sister Locs Rock: To my Sisterloc Stylists present and past, Julia, Wanda, and Calla, thank you for the blood, sweat, and conversations we had during re-tightening sessions.

Celebrity mentors: I invested in many books, audios, classes, and seminars as I researched and continuously studied to learn my craft and learn how to cultivate and monetize my gift, and learn inspirational life-changing tips to help launch me on my destined path of purpose.

Jerome W: Thank you for investing in me! Many times, I wanted to give up and forget about my purpose . . . you encouraged me to know this is bigger than me. You're an extraordinary man with a vision and pursuit to change the world! I can't wait for the world to see your invention, Jetsons watch out.

To all my family and friends, if I did not say your name and you played a part in my success—it was not my intention to neglect your name, but I thank you for playing your significant role in my life. Thanks for adding value to me. I am paying it forward and I will elevate our family trajectory!

BIBLIOGRAPHY

Fortuna, J. (2012). "The Obesity Epidemic and Food Addiction: Clinical Similarities to Drug Dependence." Journal of Psychoactive Drugs, 44(1), 56–63.

Grant, J., Potenza, M., Weinstein, A., & Gorelick, D. (2010). "Introduction to Behavioral Addictions." American Journal of Drug & Alcohol Abuse, 36(5), 233–241.

https://www.bulimia.com/topics/food-addiciton-hotline/.

National Institute of Mental Health. (2007). Study tracks prevalence of eating disorders.

National Institute of Mental Health. (2011). Most teens with eating disorders go without treatment.

Substance Abuse and Mental Health Services Administration. (n.d.). SAMHSA's National Helpline.

Yau, Y. H. C., & Potenza, M. N. (2014). Stress and Eating Behaviors.

BIBLIOGRAPHY FOR "IS AMERICA STILL RACIST?" BY GENESIS JEAN

https://www.the-independent.com/news/world/americas/us-politics/georgia-park-cannon-arrested-capitol-voting-b1822852.html

https://www.biography.com/activists/martin-luther-king-jr

https://www.usnews.com/news/national-news/articles/2021-04-12/biden-offers-condolences-calls-for-calm-in-wake-of-minnesota-shooting

https://www.post-gazette.com/news/nation/2021/04/19/derek-chauvin-murder-trial-closing-arguments-george-floyd-death-minneapolis-police-officer-black-lives-matter/stories/202104190058

https://www.youtube.com/watch?v=RGr6WOIkHyw

https://www.ft.com/content/ab3b7f0c-f163-4ebb-a392-d6dfa54d3467

ABOUT THE AUTHOR

Natashay Starr, Coach Starr, started her medical career in 1999, with a bachelor's degree in health communication. She is a certified Transformational coach and Bereavement coach, with additional studies. After working in multiple medical specialties, the world of medical marketing and sales became her livelihood, pitching and cultivating relationships with thousands of physicians. She began to work long hours with a mission to become ultra-successful, but she never realized her life was spiraling out of control.

A single mother, work-acholic, alcoholic, who felt shattered and broken, she was suffering from suicidal thoughts, diminished dreams, asinine aspirations . . . which all lead to undiagnosed depression. There is more to life than the mundane, mediocre, miserable moments that became the norm until now. When Coach Starr moved from Atlanta, Georgia, to Sacramento California, for work, the sabbatical began—no family, friends, or distractions—it was time to dissect her life. Many years later, it finally happened—her internal joy, peace, and self-love was restored and magnified. Perfectly imperfect is so freeing.

Coach Starr developed a passion to help others, and finally aligned, an internal chakra balance state of mind changed her life. After becoming a Certified Transformational Coach, inclusive of additional studies of bereavement, law of attraction, purposeful life, yoga, and meditation (she's a lifetime learner!), she became a product of turning pain into an impactful purpose. This has been a gift all of her life, enriching others and pulling out the gem God has placed inside of each of us (different gems for each person). It is a gift for her to pour outwardly since she spent time alone elevating the gem within her. It is time for Coach Starr to help you p.e.s. (purge.emerge.surge.) and transform into your higher self.

www.ingramcontent.com/pod-product-compliance
Lightning Source LLC
Chambersburg PA
CBHW060502130626
46553CB00002B/387